BUILD YOUR OWN
MOBILE
POWER TOOL
CENTERS

BUILD YOUR OWN

MOBILE
POWER
TOOL
CENTERS

John McPherson

BETTERWAY BOOKS

Cincinnati, Ohio

Read This Important Safety Notice

To prevent accidents, keep safety in mind while you work. Use the safety guards installed on power equipment; they are for your protection. When working on power equipment, keep fingers away from saw blades, wear safety goggles to prevent injuries from flying wood chips and sawdust, wear headphones to protect your hearing, and consider installing a dust vacuum to reduce the amount of airborne sawdust in your woodshop. Don't wear loose clothing, such as neckties or shirts with loose sleeves, or jewelry, such as rings, necklaces or bracelets, when working on power equipment. The author and editors who compiled this book have tried to make all the contents as accurate and correct as possible. Plans, illustrations, photographs and text have been carefully checked. All instructions, plans and projects should be carefully read, studied and understood before beginning construction. Due to the variability of local conditions, construction materials, skill levels, etc., neither the author nor Betterway Books assumes any responsibility for any accidents, injuries, damages or other losses incurred resulting from the material presented in this book.

Build Your Own Mobile Power Tool Centers. Copyright © 1995 by John R. McPherson. Printed and bound in the United States of America. All rights reserved. No part of this book may be reproduced in any form or by any electronic or mechanical means including information storage and retrieval systems without permission in writing from the publisher, except by a reviewer, who may quote brief passages in a review. Published by Betterway Books, an imprint of F&W Publications, Inc., 1507 Dana Avenue, Cincinnati, Ohio, 45207. First edition.

99 94 93 92 91   5 4 3 2 1

Library of Congress Cataloging-in-Publication Data

McPherson, John.
    Build your own mobile power tool centers/John McPherson. — 1st ed.
      p. cm.
      Includes index.
      ISBN 1-55870-380-2
      1. Woodwork--Equipment and supplies--Design and construction--Amateur's manuals. 2. Workshops--Equipment and supplies--Design and construction--Amateur's manuals. 3. Power tools -- Amateur's manuals.
    TT186.M38 1995
    684'.08—dc20
                     94-49135
                     CIP

Edited by R. Adam Blake
Designed by Brian Roeth

DECIMAL EQUIVALENCY CHART

1/64"	.015	33/64"	.515
1/32"	.031	17/32"	.531
3/64"	.046	35/64"	.546
1/16"	.062	9/16"	.562
5/64"	.078	37/64"	.578
3/32"	.093	19/32"	.593
7/64"	.109	39/64"	.609
1/8"	.125	5/8"	.625
9/64"	.140	41/64"	.640
5/32"	.156	21/32"	.656
11/64"	.171	43/64"	.671
3/16"	.187	11/16"	.687
13/64"	.203	45/64"	.703
7/32"	.218	23/32"	.718
15/64"	.234	47/64"	.734
1/4"	.25	3/4"	.75
17/64"	.265	49/64"	.765
9/32"	.281	25/32"	.781
19/64"	.296	51/64"	.796
5/16"	.312	13/16"	.812
21/64"	.328	53/64"	.828
11/32"	.343	27/32"	.843
23/64"	.359	55/64"	.859
3/8"	.375	7/8"	.875
25/64"	.390	57/64"	.890
13/32"	.406	29/32"	.906
27/64"	.421	59/64"	.921
7/16"	.437	15/16"	.937
29/64"	.453	61/64"	.953
15/32"	.468	31/32"	.968
31/64"	.484	63/64"	.984
1/2"	.5	1"	1.00

METRIC CONVERSION CHART

TO CONVERT	TO	MULTIPLY BY
Inches	Centimeters	2.54
Centimeters	Inches	0.4
Feet	Centimeters	30.5
Centimeters	Feet	0.03
Yards	Meters	0.9
Meters	Yards	1.1
Sq. Inches	Sq. Centimeters	6.45
Sq. Centimeters	Sq. Inches	0.16
Sq. Feet	Sq. Meters	0.09
Sq. Meters	Sq. Feet	10.8
Sq. Yards	Sq. Meters	0.8
Sq. Meters	Sq. Yards	1.2
Pounds	Kilograms	0.45
Kilograms	Pounds	2.2
Ounces	Grams	28.4
Grams	Ounces	0.04

About This Book

This book is both a concept and a plan. It contains many ideas together with a number of solutions and techniques. It details the way my shop is set up, a setup that evolved over 30 years.

There are complete plans and drawings for all of the basic building blocks needed to do professional woodworking in a limited space. Few readers will build everything presented here, since each reader's starting point and needs will be different. But every reader should find something useful and worth building, even if it's only a push handle or sanding block.

For those just starting to build their first shop, it will probably be a vision of the future. It takes time to acquire all the tools you will want to have someday. If you are an experienced woodworker, I expect you'll find some new ideas and solutions, as well as valuable ideas that can be adapted to your needs.

For many the dimensioning in this book will be a departure from the norm. I use decimals. I never know where to find $\frac{43}{64}$ on my scale, but I do know that .67 is somewhere between .625 ($\frac{5}{8}$) and .75 ($\frac{3}{4}$). I also use a calculator, and it's just as confused as I am. It never knows what to do with the adding of $\frac{43}{64}$ to $\frac{13}{32}$. I do, however, think in fractions, because the stock we are working with is measured in fractions. When I do a layout, the primary outline will be in inches and simple fractions of an inch. I avoid $\frac{1}{3}$" where possible. Even when I use decimals, repeating fractions are a problem. After the outline has been set, I let the dimensions fall where they may. If an inside dimension ends up being .52", then I use .52". There is no good reason to change it to $\frac{33}{64}$" or $\frac{17}{32}$". It's like telling time with digital clocks—we no longer convert 5:13 to quarter past five. If someone asks the time and we have a digital watch, we say it's 5:13.

Our calculators and computers can't adapt. However, I know from personal experience that woodworkers are bright, intelligent, open-minded people, and being bright, intelligent, open-minded people, we can learn to adapt.

Enjoy the book. I have enjoyed writing it.

TABLE OF CONTENTS

THE TABLE SAW WORKSTATION

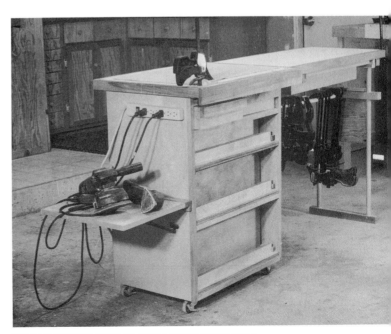

THE SANDING AND GLUING WORKSTATION

INTRODUCTION

Overview

Every woodworker needs more space, more storage and more woodworking capability. This book is written for those who want to take that next step and have the space and capabilities to tackle the really meaningful woodworking projects. Once you have the work space, you'll want to be able to use your tools right now, not after spending tedious minutes or even hours converting, setting up and adjusting for the new cutting operation. Cutting boards never takes long. What takes time—and often takes the fun out of woodworking—is the setup and establishment of the tool in order to make the cut.

The concept I'm presenting here is a simple one: Use the space you have more efficiently by using *all* the space, not just the surface space. All of your benches and fixtures can work together in support of

GUNG HO

"Gung ho" comes from a Chinese phrase meaning "working together in harmony." The phase was corrupted a little when it was used as a motto by the U.S. Marine Raiders during World War II to mean "work together," and then further changed to its current popular meaning—"overly zealous"—which is not how I would describe our new shop.

By "working together in harmony" the Chinese meant that, even if it's not your job, if you can do it and it needs to be done, then do it. I've designed the mobile power tool center with this work ethic in mind.

The serious woodworking in this shop is accomplished using the following four basic workstations and their parking structures, the power tool benches.

Router Station	With included jigs and fixtures, this station will perform all routing operations. The Porter-Cable 690 is the primary router. Provisions and designs for mounting the Sears Bis-Kit, the Dremel 231 Shaper/Router Table with a Moto-Tool, the Ryobi RE-600 and a jigsaw are also included. Most other routers can be used. Designs for specialized and general purpose fences, jigs and push sticks.
Table Saw Station	Storage for layout and measuring tools, saw blades, and miter. Designs for a tenon jig, taper jig, a 45° miter box, a crosscutting jig, a sliding crosscut box . . . and more.
Sanding and Gluing Station	This is your basic workbench. It is designed for clamping, holding and gluing the workpiece and stores numerous tools and supplies. I've also included a design for an extension table that greatly increases your shop's working surface area.
Assembly Station	This station stores portable power tools, supplies and hardware. Modular drawers can be made to serve as a drafting table module, a fine measuring-tools drawer, or a custom drawer/chest design for holding sharpening tools, electronics, hobby or carving tools.
Power Tool Benches	Designed as the parking structure for the workstation when stored. Power tool tops hold tabletop power tools.

each other, and your benches can become workstations that maximize the capabilities of your tools. Does this describe a gung ho shop?

These four basic workstations, together with a 10" table saw, can be stored in an area of less than 30 square feet of space—that is, an area of roughly 2½' x 12' or 6' x 5', which is less than the area taken up by a car. The working surface area is 60 square feet of usable space that you can further expand with storage lids, trays and modular extension tables.

There is even a design for a wood storage cart for leftover wood. This wood storage unit is a valuable addition that can also be used as a panel saw for cutting 4x8 sheets of plywood.

As your work requires greater functionality or more storage, you can build additional stations. The router workstation and the sanding and gluing station are your primary work benches. The table saw and assembly stations are designed for storage and support of the saw and of your primary stations. Finally, the power tool benches are the garages for parking the workstations. Their surfaces hold your benchtop tools.

Concept

The underlying concept I followed in designing these workstations was to maximize utility and flexibility in a minimum of space. The table saw and the router are the primary tools supported by these basic stations. These are the tools that I use the most. Bear in mind that this concept can be extended to any other primary tool or to additional tools.

Optimal utilization of space and the principles of ergonomics were the criteria I used in making the design choices. For example, the height of the workstations allows each station to be used as a support platform for other stations and for the table saw. Although every station is designed to satisfy a primary function, they are also designed to support the other stations and to offer the maximum storage area for tools and related parts.

If we look at the average tool stand as shown in the accompanying figure, we see a platform in space designed to hold some type or class of tool. The space under the platform is wasted, and the height of the platform is usually a best-fit compromise for the class of tool that will be mounted on the platform. No consideration has been given to tool or parts storage.

TOOL STAND

Most of the vertical space is wasted.

If you are going to use a particular tool, then you are also going to be using its accessory parts and supporting tools. With woodworking tools and equipment, the 80/20 rule applies: A woodworker can accomplish 80 percent of the project with 20 percent of the available tools. The workstations are designed to store at least that 20 percent of the tools that will be used 80 percent of the time and will actually hold a lot more.

Accessibility is another application of the 80/20 rule. If you have to pull out a number of tools to get at the one you want, having these tools at your workstation is of diminished value. Have the 20 percent of the tools that you use 80 percent of the time quickly and easily accessible.

Jigs and fixtures are normally built using what's available for what needs to be done at the time it is being built. The concept behind this book is to design and build these jigs and fixtures so that they will do what they are intended to do and also fit within your workstation. The rule is this: First the function, then the fit. Sometimes you can't do both, but usually you can if you plan for it when building the station and the tool. Even when the tool won't fit in the station it can be sized to fit a space that's convenient and accessible from the station.

The basic workstations can be extended and expanded easily. If you don't need to fit everything in 30-plus square feet, take advantage of your extra space. Your spouse shouldn't have the car in the garage anyway. Seriously, there are other things that must be stored; perhaps some of the ideas you see here will help you find a place to store the "other stuff" that collects in every workshop and garage.

The important thing is to take advantage of the synergy of the concept: Make the whole greater than the sum of its parts.

Design

Every design should reach for its maximum in elegance and functionality. In 1907, Alfred Dunhill said,

> It must be useful.
> It must work dependably.
> It must be beautiful.
> It must last.
> It must be the best of its kind.

I read this maxim on the cover of the Bridge City Tool Works 1992 catalog and felt it was worth posting on my wall. I have tried to capture these principles in the design of the woodworking stations presented here. Tools from Bridge City Tool Works certainly capture the essence of this maxim—even if you can't afford their tools, going through their catalog is pure pleasure.

These workstations, designed according to Dunhill's maxim, are based on my experience in laying out and building work areas that gave the maximum utility, versatility and function. I want designs that require the least amount of working space and the least amount of storage space. These designs are practical. They also, hopefully, represent an innovative approach to the building of workstations for the home or small professional woodworking shop.

I call them workstations because each is designed for a specific work function and each is the station or location supporting this function.

The approach I've followed in the design of these stations has blended both traditional and more modern methods. Along this line, you will notice that there are much faster and easier ways of building the

workstations if your primary goal is to "get functionality" as quickly as possible. You be the judge. A lot of what I recommend is cosmetic—but isn't that why we enjoy working with wood?

These designs should give the woodworker with limited space resources the facilities with which to build valuable finished products. The design reflects the techniques used in fine woodworking projects and therefore the benefit of learning the building methods and developing the necessary skills.

As part of the design concept, I typically recommend the use of better woods and materials and higher quality tools. Unfortunately, these are usually more expensive. You must be able to trust your tools and feel confident in using them. It's the same thing with materials. If the design calls for hardwood, use hardwood. Whitewood or lauan may be cheaper than what I recommend, but after spending the time necessary to build these stations, you'll quickly forget the cost difference between good and cheap materials—if you buy the better grade. Your time and effort are worth a lot more than the $20 or $30 you might save on a workstation, and you will always be able to look at the results of your efforts with pride. This is just as true here as with your actual woodworking projects. Good wood is more expensive because it works better, it finishes better, and it makes the resulting product look better.

Background

I was given my first workbench when I was seven years old. That was 55 years ago. When I was 12, my grandfather built for me a workbench that is still being used. For each of my grandsons and one of my granddaughters, I have built a workbench.

The design of these workbenches has changed very little from that of my grandfather's bench. Maybe I have done my grandchildren a disservice in passing on to them solutions that were developed for a bygone age, but I don't think so. Although I recommend departures from the traditional designs, the concepts for these new designs evolved from the traditional.

What better way for our grandchildren to start than at the beginning?

As adults, however, our needs are different. We have been through our apprenticeship. We are using powerful and sometimes potentially dangerous tools.

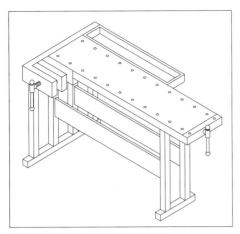

TRADITIONAL WORKBENCH

We want to get the project completed with the minimum of effort while attaining a maximum of workmanship and quality.

Looking at the pictures, reading the books, and going through the catalogs, we find that workbenches have changed very little, if at all, in the last 500 years. What has changed are the tools and the materials available with which to build our woodworking projects today.

Changes have taken place in larger modern woodworking shops. For one thing, there are no workbenches. These shops are specialized, buying from other specialty shops or factories the formed wood that they require. You will probably not find a lathe in a shop that makes kitchen cabinets. Many cabinet shops don't even make drawers or doors. These shops are factories, set up with work areas and work flows that maximize the productivity of working assets—tools—that are directly applicable to their speciality. Generally, the woodworker in these shops is not a wood craftsman so much as a skilled machine operator.

On the other hand, home woodworkers and small shop owners like me still want to make or build what we need from scratch. We are more like the woodworkers of the past, and as a result, we tend to use the same tools and benches that they used.

Unless you are building with the hand tools of these past generations, your workplace design should reflect the needs of the designs, tools and methods that you are using today. You can still build from scratch, still do it all, but do it in a way that maximizes the results of your efforts and exploits the inherent capabilities of the power tools you now own.

The workstation designs I present here have evolved over a number of years. I still use many of the designs' progenitors because I have them and they work. But the prototypes also have drawbacks that I have corrected in the later designs. My shop is now a hybrid mix of the old and the new.

In a way, I am a journeyman woodworker. Sometimes I rent shop space, and sometimes I work out of my garage. I have lots of experience in building shops and shop equipment. As you'll see, all of the workstations presented here reflect that experience.

Although the concepts behind them are not new, the designs represent new packaging and adaptations of proven methods, some of which have evolved outside the woodworking shop. For example, you may notice that some of the ideas have come from engineering workstations, from the way many small auto repair shops are organized, or from the designs of hospital carts, kitchen carts and other aids. What all of these occupational groups have in common with the woodworker is they use specialized tools, they need to take these tools to where they will be used, and they must be able to store the tools out of the way when they are not needed.

Benefits

I am not sure whether the primary benefit is having workstations that allow you to do professional work—and that can also be easily put away in a minimum of space—or having a complete set of workstations stored in the garage, along with two cars, which are (the workstations, not the cars) the envy of all your woodworking friends.

Woodworking tools are not ends unto themselves, but you can derive tremendous personal gratification from having good tools and a good working environment in which to use them. Two other important benefits that I have realized from the workstations include the positive impression that they make on my customers and the much easier job I now have in cleaning up after a day's work.

Customers like to see a clean, organized and professional-looking shop. They can relate this ambience to the work you will be doing for them. If you are building for yourself, you, too, will like the feeling of your shop and enjoy working there.

Cleaning up is a snap. You just put the tools away, blow the dust out of the stations, roll them back to their places at the tool benches, and then sweep up.

THE WORKPLACE

I've used the garage as the model for the workplace in this book. The primary criteria for locating the workplace are these:

Space	You will need 30 square feet for the saw, stations and power tool benches as well as space for one or more cars. You don't need the cars, but you will need the space. Overflow space can include the driveway. The wood storage rack requires an additional 12 square feet.
Power	Since you will be working with only one tool at a time, a dedicated 15-amp service should be all you need for your woodworking tools. If you have many lights, consider installing a separate circuit for these lights and for the other electrical appliances that you will use.
Light	Good lighting is a must. The 4' fluorescent shop units are a good, economical solution, and they're easy to install.
Ventilation	Clean air is also a must. If you are using a garage, try to establish positive air pressure in the garage, exhausting out through the garage door or some other opening. I thought I had this problem taken care of until winter came and my wife informed me that the furnace was pulling all of the dust into the house. Some redesign is always required.
Access	The garage door will normally take care of this need. Try to make it easy to get your equipment and materials in and your projects out. Don't build the boat in the basement.

Any space that has these attributes is satisfactory. One item I didn't mention above is comfort. Satisfying this need will depend on the environment you've chosen for your workplace. But if your shop is not comfortable, you will not enjoy working in it.

Sweeping up is a lot easier when the shavings and dust are primarily contained in an open area.

In studying the plans of these workstations, you will also find that other modifications and applications, focused on the areas of particular interest to you and answering your personal woodworking needs, will come to mind.

Other Requirements

In addition to your table saw and a good router, another requirement is a representative selection of hand tools and lots of clamps. You will need to be able to rip up to 24" and crosscut up to 31½". This is explained in chapter one.

You will also need the following power hand tools: a drill motor, a jigsaw, a finishing sander, and a heavy-duty orbital sander. Additionally, I have a couple of cordless drill/drivers that I find invaluable for all of my jobs.

THE TABLE SAW WORKSTATION

Purpose and Function

The table saw station supports your saw. It is designed to hold most of the tools, jigs and fixtures that you need and use when you are working with your saw. The beauty of this station is that it makes everything you need accessible; it is packaged for your convenience.

You use a number of aids and fixtures in sawing operations. It's important that these aids and fixtures be quickly accessible when needed. It's just as important to have a place to put them when they are not being used, because it's easy to clutter the saw's surface to the point where you can't cut a board. The saw station is organized to solve this problem. The tools you need are easy to get to and just as easy to put back. They're out of the way—not in the way.

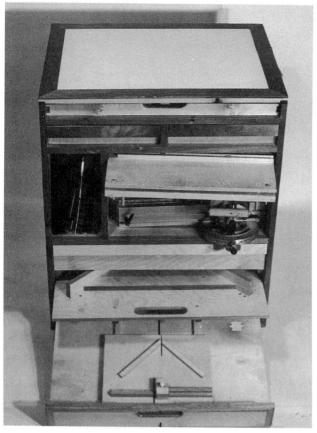

STORING THE SAW FIXTURES
Each of the saw's primary fixtures and jigs has a quickly accessible storage location.

The little jig shown stored at the bottom with the cross-cut box is a scaled-down combination of the miter jig and a 90° miter. It is used when working with small stock and workpieces found in model work.

Layout and Organization

Like all of the workstations, the table saw station is an example of parametric design. The common primary station parameters are the height of the saw and the other workstations and the ability to store or park the stations within the power tool bench outline. The objective parameter of building each station's basic carcase with a single sheet of ¾" plywood isn't quite met. You will need five 4x8 sheets of shop birch to build the four workstations.

Specific parameters for the table saw station are accessible storage for saw blades, various jigs and fixtures including cutoff boards, auxiliary fences, a taper jig, other tools and push sticks, and finally the miscellaneous parts and accessories that are used with these aids. Ideally, the design will achieve good ergonomic placement of the station's contents.

The lid of the top compartment holds the items that you will want at your fingertips. For me this includes the marking and measuring tools used with and at the saw.

The top drawers are used to store little things. Think of them as the replacements for the cigar boxes used for so many years as basic shop organizers. As we collect more and more special tools and devices, we are also collecting the little bits of hardware and parts that come with these special tools. Store these bits and pieces in the drawers.

A shelf below the drawers is divided into two compartments, one to hold the saw blades and the other to hold the miter gauge, tenon jig and other larger aids.

There is no special place for storing the rip fence. It is normally kept on the saw table or, when not in use, on the table saw station or one of the other stations. The arbor wrench also stays with the saw.

A cutoff table, small cutoff table and miter jig are sized to fit into the station as drawers. The taper jig, tenon jig and other special aids are designed to fit in their respective storage compartments. This complementary jig size/storage location is important and gives your workstation its value to you and your shop. The sliding crosscut box, which is also a drawer, can be used to hold other special fixtures. Auxiliary fences can be hung on the sides of the workstation. Typical storing of these fixtures is shown here.

TOP COMPARTMENT LID
Like the saw's jigs and fixtures, the primary small tools and aids used with the saw are both accessible and out of the way when not needed.

UPPER PULLOUT TRAY

Sometimes the workstation's top is in the way when up, and sometimes you will need to use the station as a dolly or work surface.

When you need to lower the station's top, the upper pullout tray allows all of the tools and boards that have collected to be moved as a group by pulling out the tray.

On the side of the workstation are two of the auxiliary fences used with the saw. If this space is used to store tools, the power tool bench must be wide enough to accommodate them.

The small cutoff board is stored above the miter and tenon jig shelf as a slide-in tray. The taper jig and inserts for the saw are stored in the lower tray drawer. Looking at a layout of the top lid you can see the items I have chosen to keep at my fingertips:

- Incra gauge
- 2" Try square
- 6" Try square
- 6" Vernier caliper
- 10" Featherboard

I also keep a ¾" wide 12' tape measure and a calculator handy. All of these tools are accurate and handy to use. The ability to measure accurately is paramount in the design and building of good furniture and related wood projects. To hold dimensions to a ⅟₃₂" or better

makes the difference between quality workmanship and the projects you're not allowed to bring into the house.

A tool's ease of use determines whether you will use it or not. Both the Incra gauge from Taylor Design and the vernier caliper from General Tools are examples of tools that are well designed and easy to use. In addition to its ease of use, the General Tools caliper is easy to read. Because of its yellow fiberglass-reinforced, plastic body and black lettering, even my tired, old eyes can read the scale. I almost went blind trying to read a metal rule engraved with lines separated by ⅟₆₄". This caliper also has a metric scale. With so many dimensions called out in metric measurements these days, it's handy to be able to do a quick conversion by

LOWER PULLOUT TRAY

The lower pullout tray is used for the storage of less frequently used aids, tools and jigs. It should be partitioned to fit your tools and your needs.

BOOKCASE

Imagine a simple bookcase as shown here. The sides, which hold the shelves, are complementary left and right pieces. The dadoes cut in these sides must be at the same vertical height. With the saw, it is easier to set the cut dimension for one side and then use this same setting to cut the other side. Therefore, instead of cutting all the dadoes on one side and then cutting the other side, first cut the bottom dado on the left side (16.5" in the example), and then cut the corresponding dado on the right side. Following this procedure for all of the cuts ensures that, even if the cuts were slightly off the planned dimensions, the shelves will still be perfectly horizontal and the bookcase square. This would not be the case if you had used the router and had made a mistake in marking one of the dimensions or if you had used the saw but finished one piece before cutting its complementary piece.

Another reason for using the saw is that the dado blades can be shimmed. The ¾" plywood sheet stock you buy will probably not be ¾" thick. Normally, it will be ²³⁄₃₂". This is desirable, because using either a standard ¾" setup on the saw or a ¾" bit in your router will give a good slip fit. When it doesn't give a good fit, having to make two passes

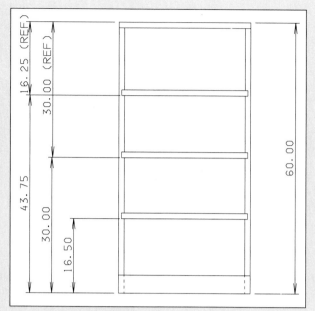

BOOKCASE EXAMPLE

with the router can get old in a hurry.

To ensure a clean-cut dado when using the saw, place masking tape over the cutting line on the bottom side of the plywood stock before making the cut. Doing this will minimize any tearing of the plywood's veneer. It also helps to have sharp, clean blades and to use an insert sized for the dado being cut.

reading across from the fraction scale to the metric scale. The Incra gauge is a little harder to read, but it does a super job of setting the height of the saw blade or the blade-to-fence dimension.

My early experiences with Universal Clamp Corporation's featherboard were not so good. For one thing, a roll pin used to secure the clamp mechanism kept slipping. However, when it worked it was valuable and easy to use, so I decided to try a new one. This new design works. The clamp screw on the new model is secured with ribs in the screw head instead of a roll pin and doesn't slip.

I have a number of try squares, but the ones I have chosen to have at the saw are the 6" and 12" models from Woodworker's Supply. These try squares have 2" blades that are both a bother and a blessing: they aren't too good for small pieces, but they're perfect for large stock and the rough and tumble environment of the saw. I keep my precision measuring tools in a separate drawer at another workstation. The steel rule I

have had for years. It is 36" long and doesn't fit the station, so I store it in the saddle of the Unifence. The saw station is designed for a 24" rule. I have seen what look like good, practical rules in the Bridge City Tool Works catalog. If you can, buy the 24" model, which fits this workstation.

A tool that belongs with every table saw is the tenon, carriage or universal jig. The name varies depending on the manufacturer, but they all perform the same function. This type jig can also be made. If you have a Craftsman saw and decide to buy, you'll need the Craftsman Universal Jig. The Craftsman miter slot is slightly under ¾". Most other table saws have a full ¾" miter slot, and you can buy the Delta Heavy-Duty Tenoning Attachment or spend less money on a Carriage Jig. Later in this chapter I present plans for building the tenon jig that I use with the Delta Unifence. You can easily adapt this type of jig to other fence styles.

While you work with the saw, the upper compart-

WORKMATE® 300 WORK CENTER

The Workmate 300 is a valuable addition to any shop, but it is even more valuable when a top and a removable wheeled base are added. The base is made from a couple of stud-length 2x4s and four casters. The top is a piece of ¾" plywood with a cleat that allows the Workmate vise to clamp the top in place. The Workmate mounted in this way can be stored under a power tool bench like any other station.

With some wood left over from the second 2x4, I made a roller block that converts the Workmate into a roller stand. When not in use, the roller hangs on the back of the power tool bench behind the Workmate. Attaching runners to the underside of the bench top allows the top to be stored above the Workmate.

Cut the 2x4s as shown here, then pin them together with ¾" dowels. Gluing the dowels to the base piece will keep them from falling out. Attach the wheels and you're in business.

This should be your first workstation. It's a good shop dolly, a roller stand, and an outfeed table for the saw. Finally, it's also a good gluing bench.

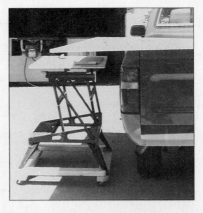

USING THE WORKMATE AS A SHOP DOLLY
The Workmate makes a handy dolly for moving large 4x8 sheets from the truck to the shop.

THE WORKMATE AS A ROLLER STAND
Leftover cuts from 2x4s make this roller base.

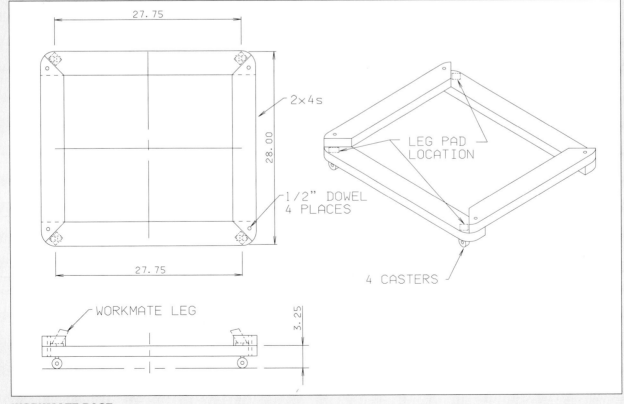

27.75

2x4s

28.00

LEG PAD LOCATION

1/2" DOWEL 4 PLACES

27.75

4 CASTERS

WORKMATE LEG

3.25

WORKMATE BASE

EXAMPLE OF CROSSCUTTING LONG WORKPIECES
Because the workstations are the same height as the saw table, they can be used to support large workpieces during cutting operations.

EXAMPLE OF RIPPING LARGE WORKPIECES
Using the sanding and gluing station as the infeed surface and two other workstations for the outfeed surfaces, it becomes a simple matter to rip a 4x8 sheet of plywood.

ment normally becomes a miscellaneous tool and parts bin and a place to stack cut boards that are part of your current project. If you want to close the lid and use the station as a dolly or work surface, you'll have to find some other place for the wood. My design incorporates a slide-out tray into the top compartment so you can move the tray loaded with the wood and your tools when you need to close the cover. How many times have you moved the same stack of wood to clear it out of the way?

Another pullout tray or drawer holds the taper jig, saw table inserts, and other saw accessories and fixtures. Partitions/dividers help you keep the drawer contents organized.

To minimize chipping and to keep yourself from being "fragged" by flying wooden shrapnel, you should use table inserts, which you can purchase or make yourself.

Shop Dolly

As a shop dolly, the saw station is both a cart for holding and moving wood and a work surface. Used in this way, it is like any of the other stations. A typical setup for handling and sawing long boards is shown here. The table saw and the assembly stations roll in any direction, while the router and the sanding and gluing stations use a pair of fixed wheels that allow only one degree of motion. Use the fixed-wheel stations as take-up tables, and use the rolling stations to move the work into the saw. If the sanding and gluing station has an extension table, it makes a very good infeed surface for the saw.

If the saw table is set with a slight rise, a bowing board will not hit the take-up station. I use a 1½° tilt, which also aids in feeding large boards onto the saw table.

It's important to remember that when you are cutting large boards, tremendous forces are being exerted against the saw blade. Always ensure that the workpiece is firmly set against the fence and never wanders from the fence. When you cut, watch the edge that is against the fence, not the cut being made or the saw blade. Resistance to the blade and the sound of the blade will also tell you whether the board is wandering. If it is, stop the saw, back up to the point just before where the wandering started, and start cutting again from this point.

Building the Saw Workstation

Getting Started

The most difficult part of building the workstations will be getting started. A 4x8 plywood sheet is bulky and can be hard to transport unless you have a truck or a friend who has one. You will probably need both the friend and the truck. Once you have the wood in the garage, you have to figure out how to make the first cut. If your workstations were already built, it would be rather easy. Some lumberyards and home improvement centers will cut plywood sheets. If they do, have them make that first long cut, cutting the sheet close to in half. This is a good first step toward making the board more manageable and transportable. The wood storage rack can also be used as the poor man's panel saw. It's not a bad idea to make the storage rack first since you will have one or more 4x8 sheets to contend with when making the workstations. Another "first" project that will greatly simplify the building of the stations is the Workmate dolly.

The purchase of a Black & Decker Workmate 300 Work Center is a worthwhile investment, one that will offer a valuable return for many years. Two stud-length 2x4s and four 1¾" (low profile) swivel casters will convert your Workmate into a shop dolly. With the addition of a ¾" plywood top, the modified Workmate will be at the standard workstation height.

The Carcase

Using the resources available to you, cut the plywood sheet into the component parts. If you use a circular saw to make some of the cuts, see if you can plan them in such a way that you can make the finishing cuts on the table saw or, if necessary, trim them with your router. The router guide described in chapter two can be used for this trimming operation. The detailed drawings, materials list, and cutting tables and diagrams for the table saw station are included at the end of this chapter.

The first step is to lay out all of the cuts that you will make on these parts and then mark the parts with their names. All of the workstations are made up of a number of right and left, top and bottom pieces. It's very easy to get confused as to what cut goes where when working with these pieces. This is experience talking. So mark where the cuts will be made, and then take the time to hold them in their final position so you can check your layout.

The rabbets and dadoes can be cut using the table saw or router, or if you have a plate jointer, you can use biscuit construction. If you do use the plate jointer, adjust the dimensions for butt joints. The construction photographs show the workstations being used to support these cutting operations. I know this isn't fair, since you don't have the stations yet, but it does let you see the power and versatility of the stations in use.

Step 1. Cut and mark the component pieces.
Step 2. Check the layout.
Step 3. Cut the rabbets.
Step 4. Cut the dadoes.

When cutting the dadoes, remember to cut the corresponding dado in each piece before cutting the next dado (see the "Bookcase" sidebar). It's best to cut the openings for the electrical connections at this time. If you plan to cut dadoes for the runners, they must be cut now, but I don't recommend dadoes for this application because you may want to move the runners sometime. Use screws instead. These runners support the jigs, allowing them to slide into the workstation as drawers.

Step 5. Dry assemble and check fit.

The fit should be a little on the loose side but tight enough to allow the station to be assembled and stay together in its final shape. This is also a good time to sand all of the pieces. When sanding, break or round-over the edges of the dadoes and rabbets. This will help in the assembly after the glue has been applied. If a joint is tight before the glue is applied it will be very tight after the glue is laid down.

Set the clamps around the piece so you know you have enough and know where you are going to place them.

The workstation carcase is glued together. There is no need to use screws or nails unless the fit is bad or

STATION ON WORKMATE
Both the size and the height of the Workmate are an advantage when gluing and clamping all of the cut pieces into a workstation. If you don't have a Workmate, use a box around 18" high.

Height of Workstation

For any one of a number of reasons, you may want to modify or adjust the height of your workstation. The dimensions given are for a workstation height of 34½". You may need a different height for a specific purpose, or the wheels you buy may be larger or smaller than the ones specified. Whatever the reason, just remember that if you do make the station taller, the power tool benches will have to grow also.

The station height as shown assumes that you will use a wheel that is 2⅜" high.

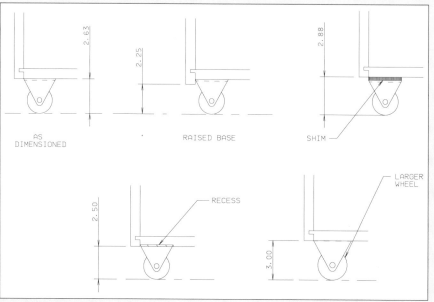

HEIGHT EXAMPLE

There are a couple of ways to lower the overall height. First, when cutting the side pieces, you can compensate for a larger wheel by setting the box dado joint higher on the side piece. This will change the size of the workstation's bottom opening, but this can be accommodated easily. In all cases this bottom opening holds a drawer of some sort, and this drawer can be made slightly smaller than the one specified.

Another way to lower the overall height of the station is to route a small recess into the bottom panel, a recess sized to accept the wheel mounting pad. I wouldn't suggest using this form of adjustment for more than a ¼" adjustment.

You can also lower the height by cutting a rabbet in the station's top. The rabbet depth will determine the resultant height of the station. Both the table saw station and the assembly station have trim strips on the top surface of the side pieces. The thickness of this strip can be used to make slight adjustments to the station height.

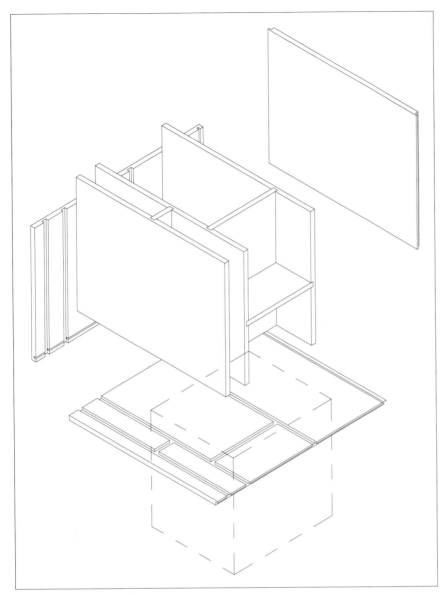

ASSEMBLY SEQUENCE

or injector and a modified, inexpensive 1" paintbrush. You can use the applicator to put the glue on and the brush to take it off. Another applicator that works well is a small (4- or 8-oz.) glue bottle. If you don't think these applicators hold enough glue, then you can play Gunga Din and use the 128-oz. bottle as your mussick.

Use the brush to clean joints after you've clamped the carcase. First modify the brush by cutting the bristles back to about ½" so that it can act more like a scrub brush. Use the brush with a damp cloth and a small pan of water to keep the cloth, brush and your hands clean when removing the excess glue.

Another aid or tool to have handy is a dead blow hammer. "Hammer to fit" still works. When the hammer fails, it's time for the pipe clamps. The Quick-Grip type clamps will hold assembled pieces together, but they cannot pull in stubborn joints. Pipe clamps may be required when assembling some of the carcases.

Start the gluing and assembly process with the back laying horizontally, dado grooves up. Try to find a stable box to set the back on (something about 18" high and small enough so that all of the back's edges are exposed for placement of the clamps). The Black & Decker Workmate 300 set to the lowest height is very handy for this type of assembly.

you don't have enough clamps to hold the carcase while the glue sets. The back of the station is an integral part of the case, acting as a shear panel to give the total case stability in three dimensions.

Step 6. Glue and clamp.

Spread the glue into the dadoes and lay a small bead along all of the edges that will fit into the dadoes. Use a good aliphatic resin glue. Most consumer yellow glues are satisfactory. Regular Titebond glue from Franklin International is probably as good a glue as you can get for gluing the station carcases, but I don't recommend that you use the Titebond II. Titebond II is waterproof, which is good, but it is also runny, and it dries with a very distinctive orange color.

A couple of handy gluing aids are a glue applicator

Assemble the parts in this order:
1. Position back.
2. Place center horizontals.
3. Add saw blade divider.
4. Slide in rear divider for saw blade compartment.
5. Add top horizontal.
6. Put in drawer divider.
7/8. Position sides.
9. Slide in bottom horizontal.

You have now completed a basic carcase for a table

TRIMMING THE EXPOSED PLYWOOD EDGES

All of the exposed plywood edges are trimmed using birch or other hardwood strips. If you want to get fancy, you can use dark contrasting wood strips. Oiled, deep red mahogany, for example, looks good with the oiled birch. The drawings for the stations show these strips and are dimensioned to show both the panel size before and after the trim strips have been glued and trimmed. If you prefer using edge banding tape, then the plywood cut dimensions must include the strip.

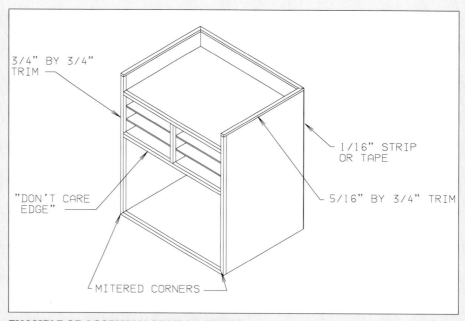

EXAMPLE OF ASSEMBLY STATION EDGES

The hardwood strips offer some meat to the edges that can't be realized with the tape. I use tape often but not where the edges will be subjected to knocking and other abuse.

The strips go on after the carcases have been assembled and glued. As mentioned, the plywood will probably be somewhat less than ¾" thick, and the strips you cut for the front will be sized to ¾" x ¾". This will give the strips a slight overhang after they have been glued down. This overhang should be on the outside of the case, as shown here.

Use tape or ¹⁄₁₆" thick strips for the back edges. You also may want to clean the back edge with the router using a mortise bit. If the case stock is a true ¾", cut your trim strips a little wider, e.g., ¹³⁄₃₂". Note that ¹³⁄₃₂" is also the width of the banding tape. The top strips on the table saw, assembly and gluing and sanding workstations call for ⁵⁄₁₆" thick strips. The ⁵⁄₁₆" measurement results when ¾" stock is cut in half. Remember, you lose ⅛" to the saw cut. You can also use the width of this strip to adjust the height of the station.

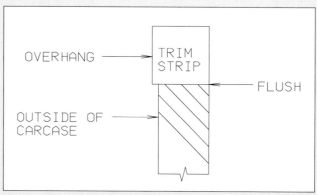

PLANNING THE OVERHANG

Trim Strip Overhang

The reason for having the overhang on the outside is that this edge can be easily sanded or trimmed later using either sandpaper, a plane, a router or a cabinet scraper. The inside edge must be flush with the plywood edge to ensure that there is no interference with the drawers that will be fitted for these openings.

The 6" Bosch variable speed, random orbital sander is ideal for this task. Keep the sanding head normal to the case surface (which is easy to do), and the protruding overhang will disappear quickly. Look for the glue line to disappear; when it does, you have sanded enough. Use 100-grit paper for this application, and use the sander's clutch/slip configuration. Remember that there must be an overhang to sand off. If there isn't, you will be sanding the plywood side's veneer. This also can quickly disappear, exposing grain going the wrong way. When you need to sand the drawer openings, the Bosch B7000 Detail Sander is your best bet.

When trimming inside edges, pick the "don't care" edge for the overhang, the edge where there will be no interference caused by a slight overhang. As shown here for the assembly workstation, the "don't care" edge is the opening of the bottom compartment. This compartment will be fitted with drawers that require at least ½" of clearance, and the ⅟₃₂" overhang will be in the noise, that is, indistinguishable from a flush edge.

It is very easy for the saw blade to burn the wood when cutting the strips. To minimize the cleanup effort, glue one of the burnt sides to the case. This will hide the burn marks and leave the other side, which also may have burn marks, exposed for sanding later. Too much burn can mean that the blade and fence are not properly aligned or that the blade is dull or dirty.

When gluing the strips in place, work from one vertical edge across the case to the other side. Don't try to glue on all of the pieces at the same time. To clamp all the pieces at once would take a lot of clamps, and it would be easy to misalign the strips. You can glue and nail the strips, but this entails extra work later when you are finishing the station.

I recommend a tung oil finish followed with lacquer or polyurethane. For a natural finish like this, the filled nail holes in light wood will show.

The trim joints can be butt joints, a combination of butt and miter joints or, if you feel very brave, all miter joints. The plans show mitered joints at the four corners. Use the miter jig described on page 20 to cut these joints.

After the glue has set, flush the edges using the methods described in the sidebar on "Trimming the Exposed Plywood Edges." If you haven't done it yet, you should now cut the electrical openings. The installation of the runners can wait until you have made the fixtures that ride on them. When installing the runners, it is sometimes handy to cut a simple template to position the runners. The width of the template is the height from the base to the bottom of the runner. The template length is

RUNNERS

Runners, nominally ¾" x ¾" strips, are used to support the various slide-in jigs.

Using a piece of scrap cut to the required runner height, one can ensure the runners are level and at the same and correct height on both sides of the station. After the upper runners are attached, the scrap template can then be cut to the height of the lower runners for their positioning.

Use screws instead of glue to attach the runners. You will probably want to make changes in the future.

that length necessary to hold the runner parallel to the base.

Position one of the upper runners with the template, then position the other side. Next cut the template to a width that is equal to the vertical height of the lower runner, and repeat the positioning and attachment process.

This leaves us with building the top and its holders, constructing the drawers, finishing the station and making the fixtures. All of the fixtures that are a part of the table saw workstation are described later in this chapter. I describe how to build the basic top in the following section and how to build the drawers in chapter three (see the sidebar on "Drawers," page 90-91).

saw workstation. One variation on this sequence that also works well is to add one side to the back at Step 2, then follow the sequence and add the second side at Step 8.

Step 7. Mount the wheels on the carcase.
It will be easier to work with the station if you don't have to carry it. The method used in mounting the wheels can be used to adjust the station's height.

Step 8. Glue on trim strips.
Take your time doing this and make sure you clean up the glue as you go along.

Building and Mounting the Top

Workstation Tops

As explained here, the tops of the table saw, assembly and sanding and gluing workstations are identically constructed. The top of the router workstation is similar yet somewhat unique, and the special characteristics of its construction are discussed in chapter two. Building the top for the power tool bench is discussed in chapter five.

Material

The workstation tops can be made from shop birch, 14-ply Baltic birch plywood, or MDF covered with a laminate like Formica. I prefer the shop birch. This material is dimensionally stable, and in the case of the table saw and assembly stations, it is light (compared to MDF) and offers a good material for attaching the various tool holders and similar items. I recommend tempered hardboard for the top of the power tool benches, but it can also be used for the workstation tops. If you use the hardboard, you must adjust the top dimensions accordingly. Some of the tops that you can see in the photographs use the hardboard and some use white Formica. I use the white tops for sketches, adding fractions and decimals and writing notes. The Formica surface is a big whiteboard and is easy to clean.

Cutting and Bonding the Top

To start, cut the material for the top about ½" oversize. This is done so that the top can be cut to its exact dimensions after the laminate or hardboard has been bonded to it. Cut the laminate so that the resulting sheet is a little larger than the top piece. Using contact cement, bond the laminate to the top. Don't worry about the material overhanging the plywood part of

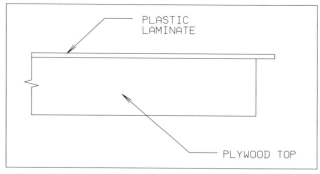

TOP PRIOR TO TRIMMING

the top; just make sure that all of the plywood is covered. Use a good quality contact cement, and follow the manufacturer's directions.

When the laminate is positioned, the cement sets immediately, and the top is ready for trimming to its final size. You will have a top that looks something like the one above.

Trimming the Top

With my saw setup, trimming the top to size is very straightforward. I have a Delta 30" Unifence mounted to a Craftsman saw. This fence has two positions as shown below.

When the small fence surface is used, the top base rides against the fence and the laminate edge can protrude over the fence surface. If you don't have a fence with this feature, you can duplicate it easily by using double-backed tape to attach a strip of wood to your

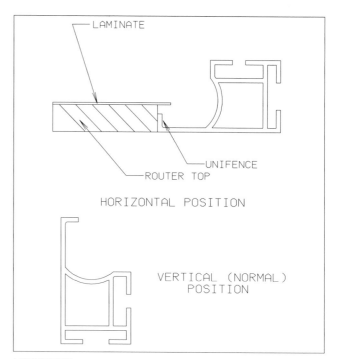

UNIFENCE

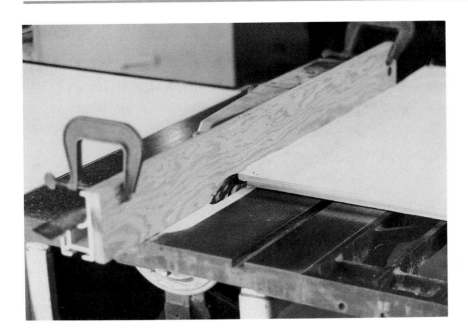

AUXILIARY FENCE FACING
When you use dado blades or shaper cutters with the saw, a wood facing for the fence will allow end cutting—for example, cutting rabbets—if you adjust the width of the cut with respect to the auxiliary fence face. The rest of the dado blade's cutting width is masked by the auxiliary fence.

fence, producing the required offset.

Cut the top to size by trimming one side and then cutting the opposite side to the final dimension. Repeat this sequence for the other two sides. The top is now ready for its border strips.

The top's border strips can be attached with glue, biscuits and glue, dowels, or a tongue-and-groove joint. I selected the tongue and groove for the table saw and router stations, biscuits for the assembly station, and dowels for the sanding and gluing station. The tongue-and-groove joints can be cut either on the saw or with the router.

When you use the saw to cut the tongues, use a hardwood or MDF auxiliary fence facing for the fence. This auxiliary fence is like a router or shaper fence. A typical setup is shown above.

Whichever method you select, plan to leave a slight trim overhang on both the laminate surface and the under surfaces.

If you have a piece of plywood that is not quite large enough for the top, you may be able to use it by making the trim wider. To have a wide border trim, it will be necessary to glue up some ¾" stock to get to a thickness that allows the overhang. The plywood and laminate are close to ¹³⁄₁₆" thick, and to have a slight overhang at top and bottom, the trim must be around ⅞" thick. The only way I know to do this, besides finding full 1" stock, is to glue up to an excess thickness and then saw or join to the required thickness. If the glue-up is well clamped, there won't be any problems with visible seams. As with the drawers, you may

want to wait until your router table is operational before finishing the top, or you may want to go with a thinner border and ignore the problem.

Whatever your solution, like the trim strips these strips will be planed, scraped and sanded flush after they are glued in place. If you don't have the slight overhang, it will be impossible to make the top flush with the border without marring the laminate surface. You can save tops with this problem by cutting a dado at the transition line between the laminate and the border. Now cut and inlay strips in the dado that will allow a height transition from the laminate surface to the border surface. This inlay strip can be from the border stock if you want to try to hide the goof, or it can be a contrasting color if you decide to flaunt the mistake. However, don't leave a protruding edge of laminate that can be caught by a workpiece that is sliding onto the table. This is particularly important for the router top.

Top Corners

The corners are mitered. The best way to measure and mark the miter line, assuming you've used a dowel or tongue-and-groove joint, is to draw the miter line on the laminate surface and then clamp each strip, with the dowels in place, in its final position and transfer the miter line to the strip. The strip is clamped to allow an accurate transfer or extension of the required miter line onto the trim strip without any gaps between the strip and the top. This method of marking is shown here.

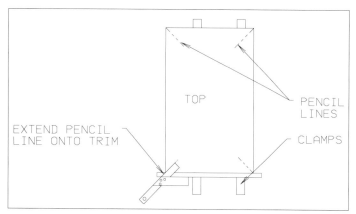

MAKING MITER CORNERS

Cut the miters, and then apply the glue and clamp the border to the top. When the glue has set, you can sand the borders flush. You now need to set the hinges and the top support.

Top Hinges

I recommend using 1¹⁄₁₆" piano hinges to attach the top to the case. To support and hold the top when in the open position, the lid support carried by Woodworker's Supply is used. These supports are available with left or right mounting and with varying torque ratings. I selected the 95- to 125-in./lb. torque for the workstation tops. Woodworker's Supply Catalog identifies these parts as 100-041 for the left mounting support and 100-040 for the right-hand mounting. Woodworker's Supply also carries the piano hinges.

The hinge can be mortised and set or attached as a strap hinge. The mortised hinge is more work and naturally looks better when installed. Two 6' x 1¹⁄₁₆" hinges will take care of all the hinge needs for the stations.

Wiring the Table Saw Workstation

The wiring of the saw station is like wiring up a shop-made extension cord. Using 8' to 10' of 14-gauge, 2-conductor/1-ground line cord, attach a 3-prong plug to one end and two double receptacles mounted in a receptacle box at the other end. Feed the cable through the receptacle opening, mount the receptacle box, and put on a cover plate.

A variation you may want to consider is to replace one receptacle pair with a flat switch. The reason for

doing this is that sometimes—for example, when cutting large sheet stock—it's hard to get at the saw's power switch. Powering the saw through the saw station will allow you to quickly turn the saw off should the need arise. I've used the flat "designer switch" in this application because a normal switch that sticks out of the side of the station can be easily broken. Cut the rear access door to fit the opening and attach with a small length of piano hinge.

Building and Using the Supporting Designs

A number of jigs and aids have been developed or modified from earlier designs to support and complement the table saw. These jigs and aids have been incorporated into the table saw workstation concept. They range from the simple but valuable push handle to the more involved sliding crosscut box and tenoning jig. Along the way, while I describe the building and use of these jigs and aids, I'll examine and discuss other supporting concepts and fixtures.

The Push Handle

Your fingers are useful. Save them. The push handle will go a long way toward helping you make difficult cuts safely. It is simple to make and should be used frequently.

Using the Push Handle. The push handle lets you cut narrower (less than 4") strips with the saw. It is

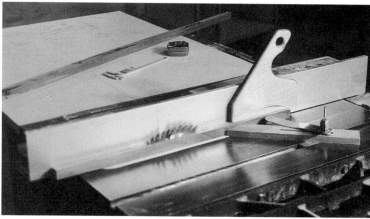

PUSH HANDLE
This push handle is designed to exert pressure both down on the workpiece and in the direction of the cut. Other push stick designs often allow the workpiece to lift when being cut because the pressure is angled at the rear of the workpiece. If you keep your hand on the handle, your hand and fingers are kept safely above the saw blade if you do slip.

often used in conjunction with the featherboard I mentioned previously. A typical setup is shown on page 18.

The push handle is designed so that, if you have your blade set at a reasonable height, your hand and fingers are always above the blade and your fingers on the right side of the handle as you pass the workpiece through the blade. Like any shop aid, the push handle works best when used properly. Keep your blade set for the height necessary to make a clean cut. The push handle's design also ensures that the board being cut will not lift as boards will with the more common push stick designs.

When you cut narrow strips, make sure you are using an insert plate in your saw to support the workpiece throughout the cut. (See section on "Saw Inserts," page 32.)

Making the Push Handle. The handle is made from ½" Baltic birch plywood or hardwood. The dimensions shown below should be adequate for you to draw the outline and cut the handle out with a band saw or a saber saw. I always start by cutting the 2" hole first and then use the small cutoff board to make the straight cuts. Use sandpaper or a round-over bit in your router to smooth out the part of the handle that your hand will be holding. This same pattern is used for a number of handles described throughout the book. You might want to consider making a pattern.

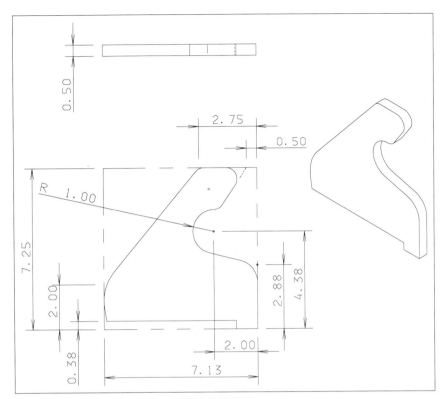

DIMENSIONED DRAWING—PUSH HANDLE

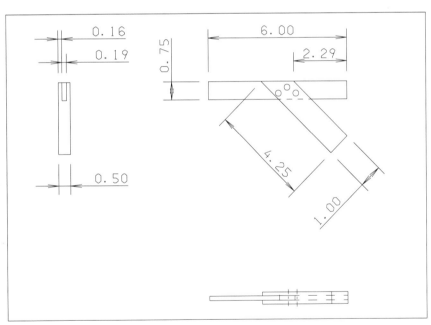

45° MITER

A Shop-Made 45° Miter

A few years ago, I made for one of my grandsons a small tool chest/bench that could be set up on the kitchen table. Included in the chest were a try square, a sliding T-bevel, a 45° miter square and a marking gauge. These tools were made of wood. One of them,

the small miter square, I found myself using as I was building the chest. It was small and light, which made it easy to use. As you may have guessed, Ian got the second miter square. I am still using the first one.

This is not a precision tool, but with only a 6" blade it doesn't have to be. It is certainly accurate enough for marking the trim and border strips used on the workstations, and it is for applications like this

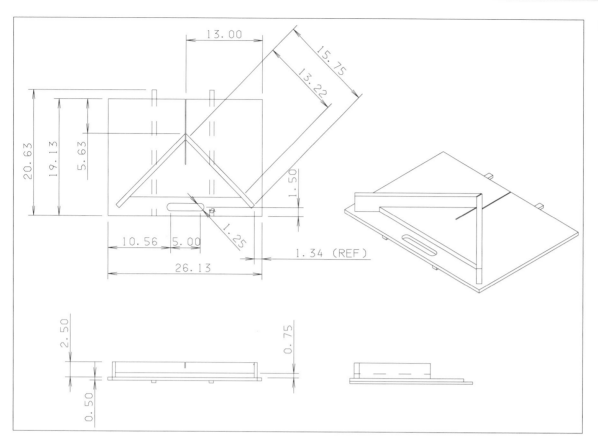

that I use it. It is small—remember, it was designed for a child's tool chest—but it will mark up to 1½" strips. For anything larger, a precision miter should be used.

Making the 45° Miter. The blade can be made from any durable ³⁄₁₆" stock, wood or plastic. Just make sure that the material is straight and true. I used some maple strips that I had left over from some long forgotten project. The handle was cut from purpleheart to simulate a rosewood handle. Again, any hardwood will work fine. To get the thickness required for both the handle and the blade, resaw from ¾" stock.

Cut the mitered end of the handle and then, using a tenon jig with the handle clamped at 45°, cut the slot for the blade. This slot should be a tight fit for the blade and centered on the handle. Work your way into the final slot width by cutting first from one side of the handle and then making the second pass with the opposite face clamped to the tenon jig. This will ensure that the slot is in the exact center. Remember, when cutting like this, that each pair of cuts doubles the amount cut from the handle. Your saw blade is about ⅛" wide.

Make your first pair of passes with the blade

approximately centered on the handle. If you were a little bit off the center, chances are you will end up with a ³⁄₁₆" wide slot.

The Miter Jig

The miter jig is a valuable accessory, and it's worth the effort to make one. Since they are relatively easy to make, you will find there will be times when making a specialized version will be worthwhile. Once I had to cut a large number of rabbeted panel mouldings for a fireplace mantel. The compound cuts had to be exact and the resultant pieces all of the same length. I made a miter jig just for this job. The 40 or so minutes it took to make the jig was paid back many times over because I didn't lose any of the cut pieces of rather expensive moulding and all of the pieces fit without trimming. I also have made a small combined miter/crosscut jig for cutting small pieces. This jig stays with the station.

The miter jig described here is really nothing new, although I do offer a few tips on constructing and using the jig. What is important is that the jig is sized to fit into the table saw station so you have a place to keep it both out of the way and handy.

Building the Miter Jig. You can either cut the run-

Table Saw Drafting Table

To use your saw table as a drafting table, use the fence as the vertical arm of an imaginary drafting arm, and use a good framing square as the horizontal arm. These tools, together with a large 45° triangle, will allow you to do accurate layout either on the workpiece or on paper. Tape paper to the saw table surface just as you would to a drafting table. When using paper, look out for the miter slots.

The following set of drawings illustrates how to use the saw table as a drafting table.

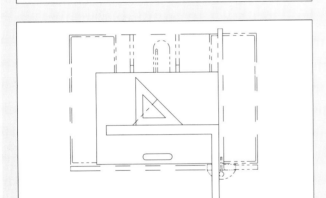

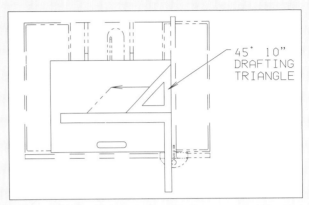

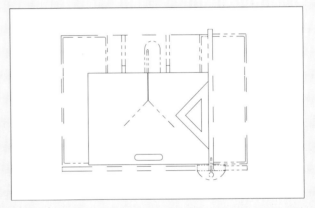

USING THE SAW FOR LAYOUT

ners from hardwood or purchase Incra Miter Slider runners, available from a number of sources. When you purchase the Incra runners, you also get a set of jig plans for applications using the runner. As I mentioned earlier, Incra products are worth owning, and these plans are no exception. For the base, use ½" Baltic birch plywood. Cut the base to 19⅛" x 26⅛". (If you are using the Incra sliders, the board should be cut 18" wide.) The actual dimensions are not as important as making sure you have cut an accurate rectangle. Also, remember that the 26⅛" length is dimensioned for sliding into the table saw station.

For the dimensions given, the diagonals should be 32⅜" long. Use diagonals for checking the square of any large rectangle. This is just like when you make rectangular boxes with square corners by using the Pythagorean theorem to calculate the length of the diagonal and then making sure that the box diagonals are equal and of the required length. If the diagonals are equal, you have a square.

Cut the fence support from ¾" plywood. The Incra instructions say to use two pieces of ¾" ply for the fence supports, but I have always made my miters with one because it allows a wider purchase for clamps to hold stop blocks or the workpiece to the miter fence.

The cutting and placement of the fence support are critical to building the miter board. Make sure that you have a square (90°) corner. This corner will be used to position the fence pieces. The large cutoff box is used to cut this piece. What you want is a perfect square or, at a minimum, a perfect right-angle corner. If you use the saw's fence you must start with a piece of wood that has a 90° corner; otherwise you can get a

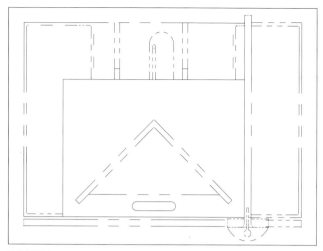

POSITIONING THE BASE

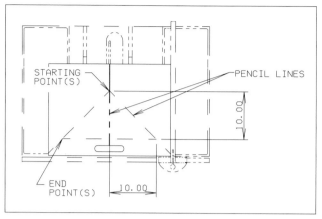

FENCE LAYOUT

perfect parallelogram but not necessarily a perfect square. You need a 90° miter cut.

Once you've cut your fence sides, you are ready to assemble the jig. The fence sides can be made from good plywood stock, which will eliminate any hard bowing problems you might experience using hardwood.

To assemble the workstation miter jig, place the runners in the saw's miter slots, position your fence for a 13" cut, and place the base on the saw table against the fence. This is shown above.

Next, screw the runners to the base. It's a good idea to sand the bottom of the base prior to this step, as you want the base to slide smoothly on the saw table surface. You can also glue the runners to the base, but you might want to wait until you are finished with the miter jig's assembly before doing this. If you want to screw the runners from the bottom, tack the runners to the base with small brads, turn the base over and put in the screws. Add the glue when ready. The screw holes become the alignment pins.

After attaching the runners, raise the saw blade and slide the jig forward, cutting into the base about 5½" to 6". Using a straightedge or framing square and a pencil, extend each side of the saw cut as shown above.

Also shown in this figure are the lines for the placement of the

fence support. These lines are constructed by measuring down the extension of the saw cut 10" (starting point), and then measuring out on both sides 10" (end points). Now connect the starting point to the end points. The best way I know to lay out the horizontal lines is to use the table saw as a drafting table. This is one of the reasons that the miter base was cut as a true rectangle.

Using the saw as a layout table, you can use the framing square to mark off the horizontal legs of the 45° triangles for placement of the fence support. Use the saw fence and the 45° triangle as aids to ensure that the fence support is properly placed and to hold it in place while fastening it to the base. This setup is shown below.

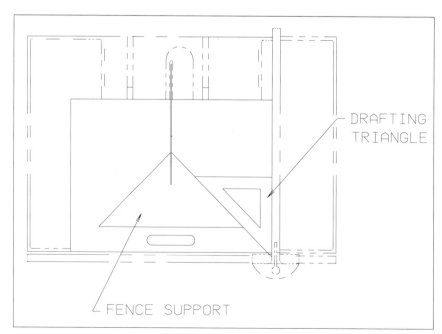

PLACEMENT OF FENCE SUPPORT

Attach the fence arms to the base with screws through the bottom of the base or drill down from the top. It's always a good idea to keep the surface that positions the workpiece clear of holes or obstructions that could affect the use of the tool. This is why the fence arms are not directly attached with screws to the fence support. You should, however, use the fence support to ensure that your fence arms are perpendicular to the base.

Checking the Miter Jig Accuracy. When making the miter cuts in the workpiece, cut the mating miters on the left and right sides of the jig. If the jig's fences are at 90°, or square to one another, then your miter cuts will give a square corner, even if the fences are not perfectly aligned. For example, you may have a 43° miter and a 47° miter, the sum of which is 90°. To check that everything is aligned, cut four 12" to 18" strips all on the left side, lay them on a flat surface, and see if you end up with a square.

Using the Miter Jig. The miter jig can cut a miter in a piece held vertically up to the height limit of the saw (approximately 3¼") less the thickness of the base (½"). When the board is held flat on the jig, you can cut a board 4" wide. Since the height of the fence is 2", the jig can accommodate small- and medium-sized crown moulding. It's easier to cut crown moulding this way than to try to figure out how to position the workpiece so you can cut the correct compound miter with a chop saw.

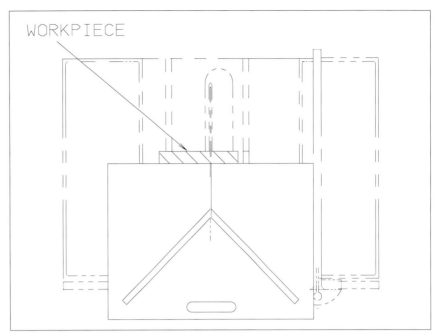

CROSSCUTTING WITH THE MITER JIG

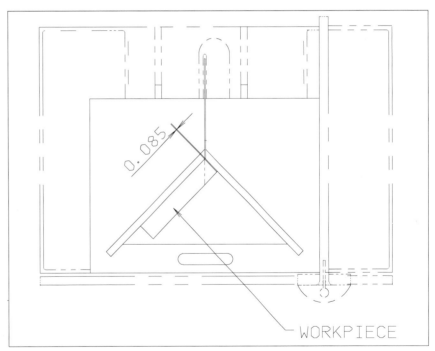

CUTTING MITERS

As I stated earlier, the miter base must be square for two reasons. First, it will aid in the layout and construction of the jig. Second, when using the miter jig, you very often need to cut a board or square the end of a board. Taking your jig off the table and replacing it with the saw's miter is inconvenient and time-consuming. Since the front edge of the miter jig is square and perpendicular to the saw blade, this edge can be used as a 90° miter. You can just hold the workpiece against the base face and cut. This is safe as long as you observe the normal safety precautions you would for any cutting operation.

Another miter cutting operation that can be done on the jig is to use the inside of the fence to hold the workpiece and the opposite fence as a stop.

The workpieces are cut square to a predetermined length, and the miter cut is made with the miter jig.

When cutting miters like this, .085" of the wood's length will be lost at each end. Therefore, the predetermined length should be .17" longer than the required finished length. I must add that this is not the proper use of the miter box. The work should be supported so that the force of the saw blade when cutting the workpiece is pushing the workpiece against, not away from, the fence. These reservations notwithstanding, this is a quick and easy way to turn out a mitered frame.

Believe me, it takes longer to read about miter jigs than to build them.

The Cutoff Board

A cutoff board is very handy for making cuts that cannot use either the fence or the miter gauge. It represents a practical application of the Theorem of Procrustes. A cutoff board should be made so that the right edges of the board and the clamp are the alignment guides. A line drawn on the odd-shaped piece to be cut is aligned with the edge of the clamp and clamped in place. The cutoff board and the clamped piece are then pushed through the saw. The following figures show how this is done.

Making the Cutoff Board. Make the width of the base and the clamp bar slightly (about ½") oversized and then make the final cut with the cutoff board runner placed in the miter slot. This ensures that the

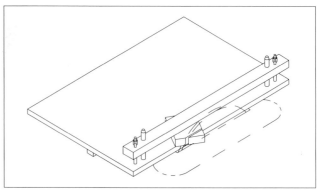

THE CUTOFF BOARD

right edge is the cutting line. Therefore, the runner that fits into the saw's miter slot must be wobble-free (this is a good application for the Incra Slider), and the clamping bar must also keep its alignment without any play. That is the reason for the alignment pins. Using the clamping hardware as alignment pins doesn't work too well since there aren't the bearing surfaces to work with, and the screw threads tend to open the hole with use.

The size of the board depends on the type of work you are doing and often on how big a piece of scrap plywood you have around. Remember that you are usually cutting workpieces at some extreme angle that can make a narrow board very wide. The size shown here is on the large size for a cutoff board and will handle most of the cuts you will want to make. It is sized to fit in the workstation as a slide-in drawer.

All of the dimensions shown are for my table saw.

CUTOFF BOARD—DIMENSIONED DRAWING

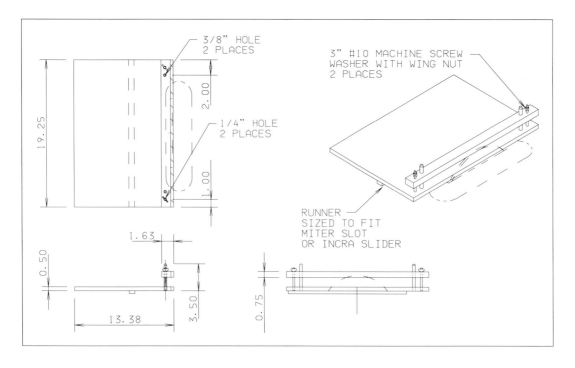

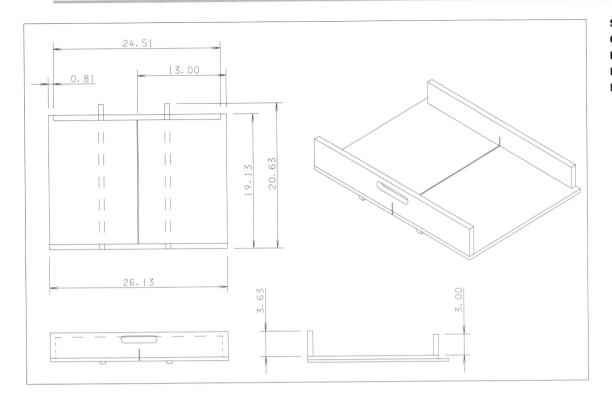

Check your saw's miter slot-to-blade distance and then modify the dimensions accordingly.

Make sure that you leave adequate clearance for the clamping bar's wing nuts to clear the saw blade.

Although the square of the base is not critical for this design, it is always a good idea to square your stock before assembling. To build your cutoff board, first cut the pieces, drill the holes in the clamping bar, and place the runner in the miter slot. Lower the saw blade below the table surface and set the fence about ¼" away from the right side of where the blade will be in the raised position. Next, position the base over the runner and against the fence (this is why you square the base) and screw it to the runner. Position the clamping bar against the fence and use it as a template to mark the clamping hardware hole positions in the base.

It's easier to use the cutoff board if the clamping screws are permanently attached to the base. You can epoxy them in place or you can drill a tap-sized hole for the screws and then thread them into the base. Do both. Make sure your countersink on the far side of the base is deep enough so that the head of the screw is slightly below the bottom surface of the base.

Having completed these steps, clamp the clamping bar to the base and match drill the alignment pin holes. Put some glue in the base holes from the bottom side, and then put the dowel pins in from the top

side. Hopefully, this will ensure that you have not glued the clamping bar to the base.

This is also a bad time to realize that the alignment pin holes are a force fit and not the required slip fit. You will find that most dowels are a little undersized, but it's better to check before you start gluing. If the dowels are too tight, chuck one of them in a drill motor and then spin the dowel in its hole. Repeat for the other hole. If this doesn't work, drill a $^{17}/_{64}$" hole or sand the dowel until you have a good slip fit.

When the glue has dried, and with the clamping bar still clamped in place, set the board assembly in the miter slot, raise the blade, and cut the right edge. You now have a completed cutoff board that is far more flexible than Procrustes' bed.

Using the Cutoff Board. The side support used in the power strip box of the assembly workstation represents a good application for the cutoff box. This side support was used in the earlier example. The cutoff board can also be used to cut the rabbets in the end plates of the power strip box.

The Sliding Crosscut Box

The sliding crosscut box is used to crosscut large boards that cannot safely or accurately be cut with the saw's miter gauge. The fence support just discussed illustrates the type of cut that is best done with this box. The box's construction is similar to that of the miter jig, and again, the care taken in its construction will determine the accuracy of the tool.

In *Tage Frid Teaches Woodworking, Book 1 Joinery*, Frid describes the making of a "Jig for Sawing Square Crosscuts." He discusses checking the jig for squareness and sums it up by stating, "I was lucky the first time, and I was very proud." I believe him. Unfortunately, I often don't get it right the first time and look for some help from my tools and fixtures to get that first-time success. The crosscut box is no exception.

The accuracy of the box is just as important as the accuracy of the miter gauge or the alignment of the fence. Your goal is to construct a two-sided rectangular box, the sides of which must be normal or perpendicular to the saw's miter slots and the path of the saw blade. Sounds easy, doesn't it? Let's see how easy it is.

Building the Sliding Crosscut Box. Step one is cutting the base panel to size, using ½" Baltic birch plywood. Here, again, we want a rectangle, not a parallelogram. The diagonal in this case is 32⅜". Place the runners in the miter slots, set the fence for 13", and position the base against the fence over the runners.

Now screw the base to the runners, making sure that the base remains in contact with the fence. Again, if you want the runners screwed in from the far side, tack the runners in place with brads.

The next step, attaching the front and rear fences to the base, can be done a couple of ways. If the base is a perfect rectangle, then you can use its edges to align the fences. Check this with the framing square placed against the saw's fence and along the side of the saw itself.

Pull the base out so it hangs over the front of the saw table, then clamp the front fence in place. Use the framing square for alignment. Get down on your hands and knees and drill the screw pilot holes through the base and into the fence. Now attach the screws. Turn the board around, reset your fence, and do the same thing for the rear fence.

You now have a dry assembly that is sturdy enough to be used to check the accuracy of the cut. You should be very happy. If you are, glue it together and then check it again.

The Tenon Jig

The tenon jig I have owned for many years can only be set for 90° and 45° cuts. To make cuts of some other angle, I have had to jury-rig something. After jury-rigging far too many times, I finally broke down and made a tenon jig that would handle cuts between 90° and 45°. This jig rides on the Unifence. It may be necessary to modify the design to fit the particular fence you are using.

Building the Tenon Jig. The jig has three parts—the slide, the cradle and the clamp(s)—and rides on the fence. The most critical aspect of its construction is assuring its smooth, wobble-free movement along the fence. Before cutting and making the actual jig, make the slide that will hold the jig to the fence. This will help you work out the nuances of your fence attachment design. Use ½" and ¾" birch ply to make the jig.

The slide rides on the fence as shown on page 27. Use screws to hold the four pieces together until you are happy with the fit. When rounding the handle it will be easier to disassemble parts of the slide if you use a round-over bit in your router. After you complete the shaping, glue the slide parts together.

The cradle together with the

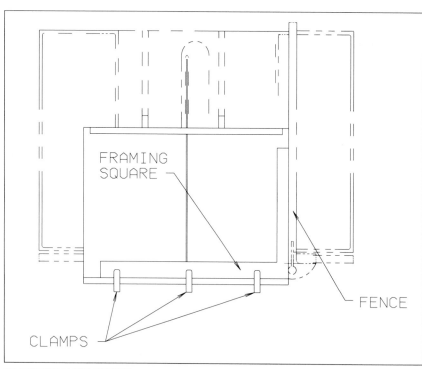

FRAMING SQUARE

CLAMPS

FENCE

CLAMPING THE FENCE

clamp holds the workpiece and is held to the slide with a recessed elevator bolt or carriage bolt. Making the knobs is described in chapter two, "The Router Workstation."

The workpiece clamp is held to the cradle with a standoff bolt. A ¾" dowel is used as the standoff. The handle allows the bolt to be secured to the cradle without interfering with the fence.

After assembling the tenon jig, match drill alignment holes through the cradle to the slide at 90°, 60° and 45° angles. Use a dowel or an axle peg (available from most of the mail-order houses) to hold the cradle at the selected angle. For angles other than 90°, 60°, or 45°, use a protractor to set the angle, then clamp the cradle to the slide.

Using the Tenon Jig. Clamp the workpiece onto the jig, set the saw blade height, and then position the fence for the required cut. When making tenons or centered dadoes, you normally turn the piece in the jig, leaving the fence position fixed. For other second cuts, moving the fence is easier.

TENON JIG

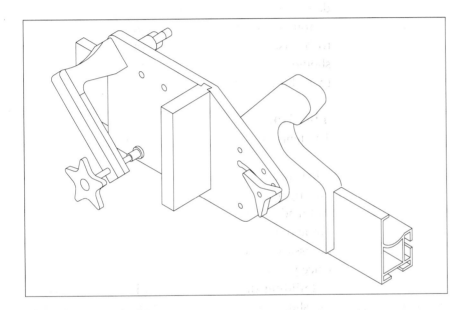

TENON JIG SLIDE

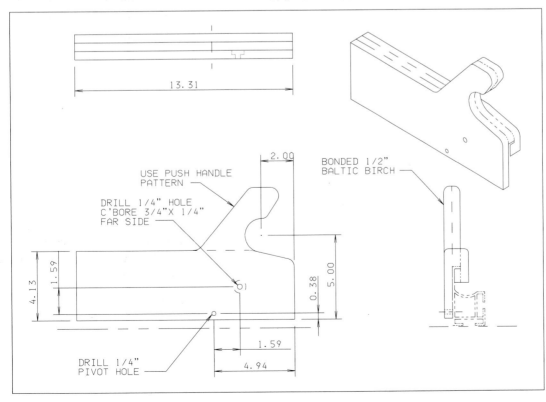

**TENON JIG
CRADLE**

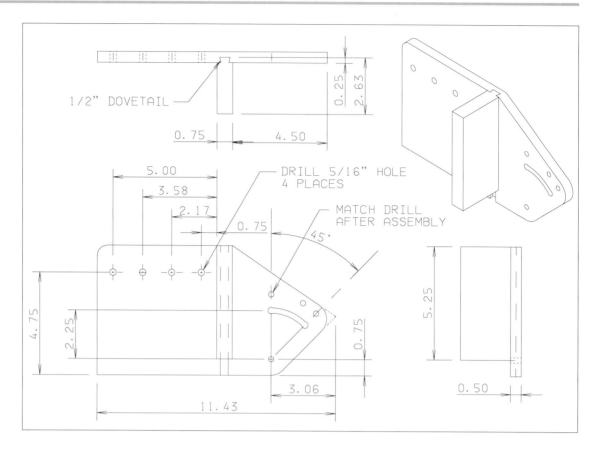

**TENON JIG
CLAMP BOLT**

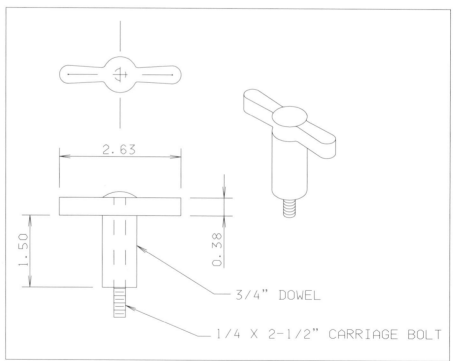

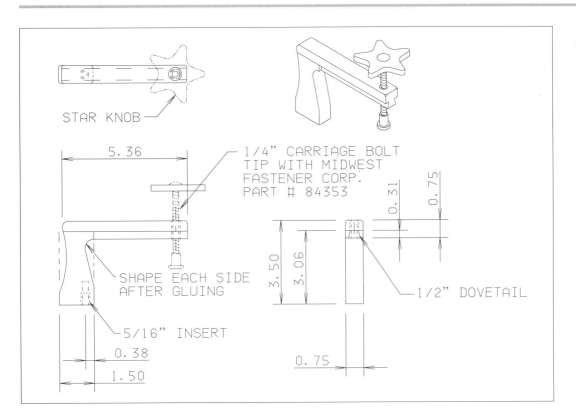

STAR KNOB

5.36

1/4" CARRIAGE BOLT
TIP WITH MIDWEST
FASTENER CORP.
PART # 84353

0.31

0.75

3.50

3.06

SHAPE EACH SIDE
AFTER GLUING

1/2" DOVETAIL

5/16" INSERT

0.38

1.50

0.75

SETTING THE TENON JIG'S VERTICAL
Use a quality try square to set the jig's vertical with respect to the saw table surface before drilling the 90° alignment hole. Next, set a baseline on the handle from the pivot hole to the 90° hole, then lay in the 45° and 60° hole centers using drafting triangles or a compass.

The Taper Jig

A taper jig is required for making tapered legs and similar cuts. When working with large stock, like the tapered edge of a large panel, a one-time jig usually is best. For tapered chair and table legs, a permanent, variable taper jig is worth having. The jig I describe here will handle lengths of 24" and tapers of from 0° to 15°. It can be used with the fence positioned on either the saw blade's right or left side.

Building the Taper Jig. Use Baltic birch plywood for the taper jig. You can obtain the necessary stock thickness by gluing up any combination of standard sheet thicknesses. The drawing shows the minimum stock thickness required for the design to work. You can use thicker stock but not thinner. Note that the dimensions are referenced from the inside surfaces and from the hinge pivot. When using thicker stock, lay it out this way. I mention the thicker stock because if you use what you have available, your combined stock may not add up to 1.13", e.g., three strips of ⅜" material. You can also have the legs of different widths; the design will still work.

Look ahead to chapter six for the jig recommended for cutting parts like the pivot arm.

Using the Taper Jig. After preparing the stock, set the taper angle, position the fence and make the cut. I always pencil in the cut line on the workpiece to help

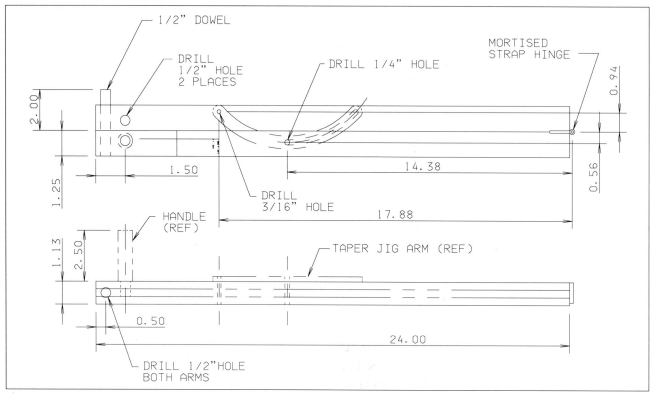

TAPER JIG—DIMENSIONED DRAWING

check the setting. Hopefully, if the position of the fence or the angle setting is off, you can stop in time to save the piece. Or you can build your table legs with 7° tapers instead of 8° tapers.

Use the tangent of the angle to set the taper. (See the sidebar on "Tangents.")

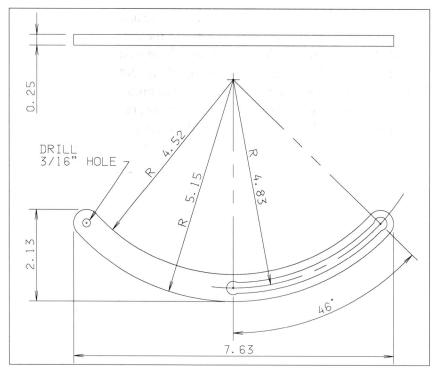

TAPER JIG PIVOT

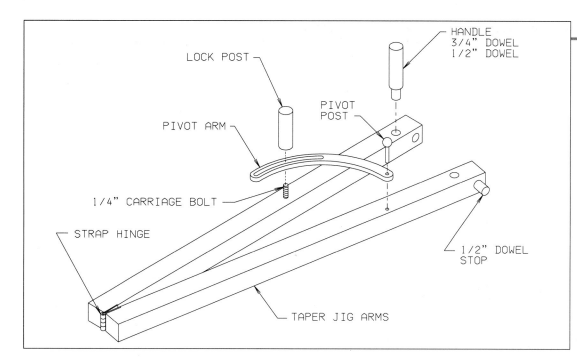

LOCK POST

PIVOT ARM

PIVOT POST

HANDLE
3/4" DOWEL
1/2" DOWEL

1/4" CARRIAGE BOLT

STRAP HINGE

1/2" DOWEL STOP

TAPER JIG ARMS

TANGENTS

By marking a point (and drawing a line) either 10" or 20" from the hinge pivot, you can use the tangent of the angle to quickly set the degrees of taper. If you write the tangents from 1° to 15° on the taper jig bar, you won't lose them.

To set the degrees of taper using a try square and scale, set the distance between the arms to the tangent times 10 or 20, depending on where you marked the arm. The reason for using 10" or 20" from the pivot is so that you're not forced to multiply some more awkward number like 7½ times the tangent. Setting the angle at 20" from the pivot will give you a very accurate setting.

Degree	Tan	10 in	20 in
1	.017	0.17	0.34
2	.035	0.35	0.70
3	.052	0.52	1.04
4	.070	0.70	1.40
5	.087	0.82	1.74
6	.105	1.05	2.10
7	.123	1.23	2.46
8	.141	1.41	2.81
9	.158	1.58	3.17
10	.176	1.76	3.52
11	.194	1.94	3.89
12	.212	2.12	4.25
13	.231	2.31	4.62
14	.250	2.50	5.00
15	.268	2.68	5.36

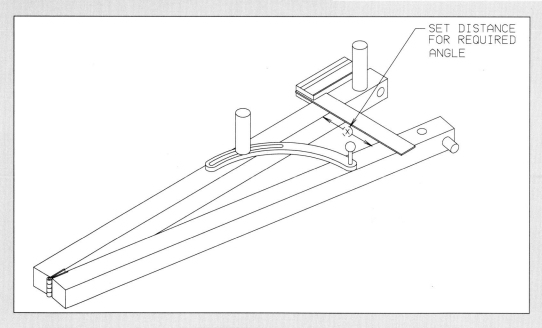

SET DISTANCE FOR REQUIRED ANGLE

Saw Inserts

If you have a Delta saw, you can buy precision table saw inserts from a number of sources. If you have an old Craftsman, as I do, you're out of luck. Using inserts that are sized for the blade or blades being used is safer and allows for better cuts in the workpiece. If you can't buy the inserts, you have to make them.

The plans here are for an insert used with a Craftsman table saw that was discontinued over 30 years ago. Few readers may have this model saw, but I hope that the plans and techniques I used to build these inserts will help you in solving the needs of your own saw. If you can buy blank inserts for your saw, do so; they will probably be better than what you can make. To be honest, I have never bought an insert, so I really don't know if this is true.

The insert for the old Craftsman is a flat .125" plate with spring clips mounted on the underside at each end. The shop-made insert will not have those spring clips, so the fit of the insert to the saw top must be snug.

The bottom view of the shop-made insert shows the rabbeted ledge. This ledge results from using ¼" Baltic birch plywood for the insert material, which is stronger than the ⅛" material.

After the insert material has been roughed out with a saber or band saw, it will be trimmed to its final size with the router. You can make a router pattern for this trimming from ¾" MDF. To make the pattern, cut a slightly oversized piece of MDF and attach it with screws or double-backed tape to the saw's insert plate. Using a pattern bit and the saw's plate as the pattern, trim the MDF to size (see the figures).

The saw's insert plate is too thin to allow the pattern to be cut in one pass. Since there is always a relief between the pattern bit's roller guide and the cutting edge, the first pass cut will leave a ledge that must be removed. To get rid of this edge, remove the metal insert plate, turn the MDF pattern over, and trim the edge away using the trimmed surface of the MDF as the pattern for the bit.

Check the fit of the pattern to the saw. You may need to remove a little material. If you do, use a sanding block as described in chapter four. You can now make inserts using this pattern. Now that you have gone to all this trouble, I'm going to recommend another jig that will make the pattern easy to use and allow you to make a number of blank inserts. This jig, which is called a pattern box, is generic so that it can

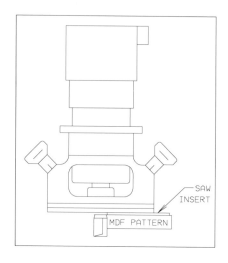

TRIMMING THE MDF PATTERN

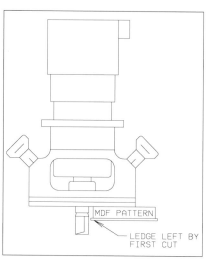

TRIMMING THE LEDGE

be used for many applications where you want to cut a number of identical pieces. The pattern box uses dowels as alignment pins. In applications where you don't want holes in the workpiece, use double-backed tape.

To build the pattern box, cut a base of the size needed and border with strips of MDF. This border merely supports the router, so only the height is important. Sandwich the slightly oversized insert material between the MDF pattern and a second piece of MDF used as a spacer. Then center the sandwich of MDF and ¼" plywood in the pattern box with the alignment dowels. The pattern box is shown on the next page.

Make the first cut using a pattern bit in the router, then turn the sandwich over and make the rabbet cut using a rabbet bit. The depth of this second cut is critical; it will determine the flushness of the resulting insert.

Having made the blank inserts, you will need to cut the opening for the saw or dado blades. The easi-

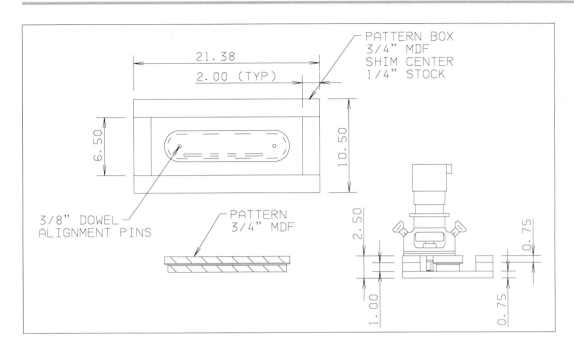

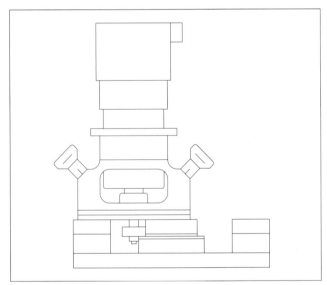

PATTERN BOX—SECOND CUT

est way to do this is to have the blade that will be used with this insert in the saw, lowered below the saw table surface. Place the insert in the cavity, and then, using a scrap 2x4 or an auxiliary fence clamped to the fence, bring the fence over so that it holds the insert down. Make sure the fence is not over the saw blade. Turn the saw on and raise the blade, thereby cutting the blade opening.

Save the basic MDF pattern; you may need it again.

Building the Tool Holders

Now you must make the holders for the tools you have decided to have at your fingertips. The instructions and drawings for the holders contained here are for the tools that were discussed previously. Treat these instructions as ideas for solving your particular needs. There are also some comments on things to avoid when making holders.

Positioning, Cutting, and Assembling the Tool Holders. The trick to designing holders is to make them simple; a good design allows a tool to be easily placed into and removed from its holder. Since the top of the workstation opens, the tools must stay in place both when the top is horizontal and when it is vertical. For the normal tool holder, gravity works for us. In this case, it's working against us—so much for fair-weather friends.

Whenever possible, try to make the holder so that the tool does not need to be adjusted to fit into it. You will see that I break this rule occasionally but only when no other solution works or works as well. I use magnets as holders when possible. For nonmagnetic materials such as brass, aluminum, plastic and wood, Velcro often becomes the magnetic force.

Your ability to easily grasp and remove a tool when it's in its holder should govern a tool holder's design. You will notice that the try square holders expose the edges of the try square, allowing the fingers to easily grasp the blade for removal. Standoffs are also used to position the tool away from the mounting surface. When you're working with wood a lot you won't have the fingernails to pry the tool out.

Where you position the tool and how the tool is oriented depend on such factors as where the station will normally be with respect to the saw, whether you

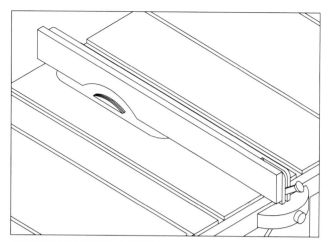

CUTTING BLADE OPENING

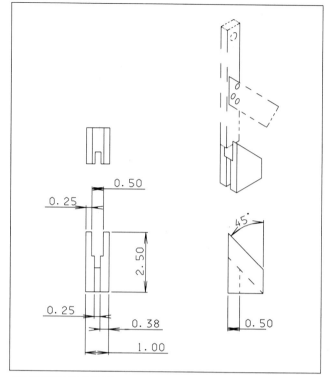

45° MITER HOLDER

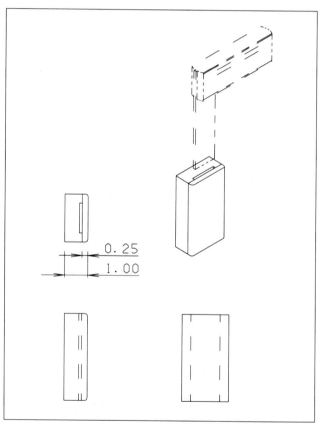

ALTERNATE TRY SQUARE HOLDER

are left- or right-handed, and where there is room for the tool. Often the ergonomics loses out in the end to wherever there is room for the tool.

I am right-handed but reach for a tool with my left hand and then pass it to my right hand. I reverse the sequence when putting the tool away. As a result, most of my tool holders have a left-handed orientation. Before you set the holders, see what feels most comfortable to you. Treat the pictures and diagrams as schematics that show what, not necessarily where. With this in mind, remember that you may want to build mirror images of the holders shown here.

As a final note on designing holders, follow the rule "first the function, then the form," which means this: First make it do what it is supposed to do, and then work on making it simple and pretty. Remember, Dunhill said first, "It must be useful," and then he said, "It must be beautiful."

The 45° Miter. Appropriately, the 45° miter fits in a holster. When making this holster, start with stock that is at least 6" long. You will need this length to make the cuts safely. Glue-up scrap and resaw to get the 1" thickness. Make the 45° cut and then, using a tenon jig, cut the 45° dado. Next cut the straight dado, and then cut to the final 2½" length. The left-right orientation will depend on which side is against the workstation's top.

Try Square Holders. The try square holders are sized to fit the particular try square being stored. The method shown here will work with any try square that has a steel (magnetic) blade. The dimensions are for the large try square. If your try square is made from nonmagnetic material—for example, rosewood and brass—use the alternate design shown.

For the magnetic variety, the magnets should be

mounted so that their surface is slightly proud of the mounting surface. The magnets used in this design are the $^{11}/_{16}$" ceramic type. They are .20" thick. Use a ¾" Forstner bit and drill a hole about ⅛" deep to accept the magnet. Then, using quick-set epoxy, glue them in place. The magnets can be ordered from Woodworker's Supply. They are carried under the catalog number 814-666 and come 25 to a package. They are also available from Master Magnetics, Inc., Castle Rock CO 80104, under part number 07003.

Incra Gauge Holder

It almost sounds like Jimmy Durante's song "Inky Dinky Do." Jimmy Durante had a large nose, and the Incra gauge has a large knurled knob. This knob is used to hold the gauge.

One easy way to make the slot that the knob slides into is to use a key slot cutter. Another way is to first cut the large dado, then bond a thin strip to this piece and, when the glue has set, cut the small dado opening. You may also have to resaw or sand to get the right thickness of the lip.

Hold-Down Push Handle Holder

This holder is quickly made from a piece of ¾" stock. When cutting the deep dado, try to end up with a width of cut that will offer some slight resistance to the handle, just enough to allow the handle to stay in place. The top edges of my holder after I cut the dado slot bowed in slightly, giving a perfect friction fit.

Caliper Holder

Belts and suspenders, Velcro and magnets. Both are used in making the caliper holder. The depth rod of the caliper is steel, and to keep the end of the caliper from flapping in the breeze, a magnet holds it in place. The Velcro on the caliper is out of the way and won't cause any problem or bother when you use the caliper.

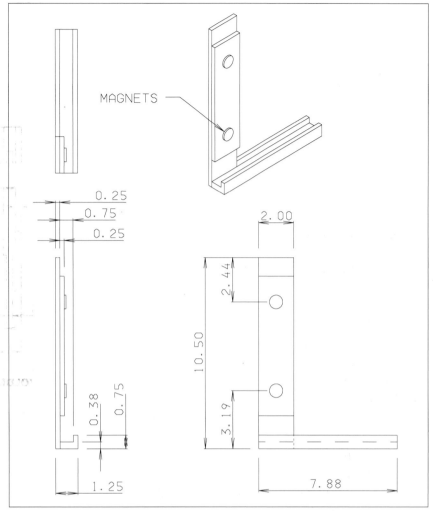

MAGNETIC TRY SQUARE HOLDER

Featherboard Holder

Some things are never easy. Mounting the featherboard was not easy. The real culprit was the height of the saw station's top compartment. To solve this seemingly insurmountable problem, I cut a dado in the station's top. At the bottom of the dado slot, I mounted a holder. It works, but if you don't want to bother, just keep the featherboard in a drawer. I bothered because I wanted the board accessible and because I wanted to solve the problem. Attaining elegance is seldom easy.

Finishing the Workstation

I strongly recommend that you finish the workstation and its accessories. It's good experience, and a slick, smooth surface is easier to keep clean.

Normally it's best to completely assemble the station and then take it apart to do the finishing. This way if there are any butch plates required or holes to be filled, these corrections can be made before apply-

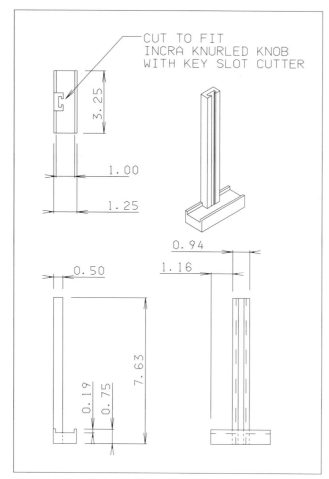

CUT TO FIT
INCRA KNURLED KNOB
WITH KEY SLOT CUTTER

INCRA GAUGE HOLDER

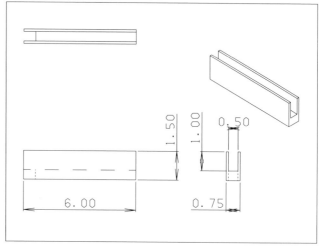

PUSH HANDLE HOLDER

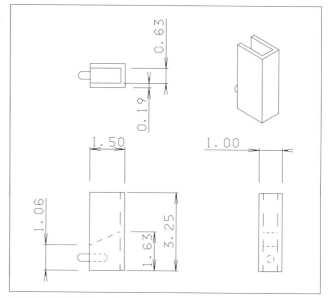

FEATHERBOARD HOLDER

ing the oil and coating finish. There's one nice thing about oil: If you run into a spot where you didn't remove all the glue (you'll see it when you put the oil on), you can sand it away with wet-dry sandpaper as you find it. In fact, using 200- or 300-grit wet-dry paper to apply the oil works fine, but a saturated rag is faster. Use both. As soon as you have oiled a part, wipe it clean of excess oil. Don't let the oil thicken on the oiled piece. Wait three days before finishing the part with either lacquer or polyurethane.

To start this part of the finishing process, sand the part smooth and clean with 220- or 280-grit paper. Wipe the dust away with a tack cloth or a damp chamois. A damp chamois is best, since it can be cleaned as you go along and reused for many years. Use the chamois just like you would when washing your car.

For a lacquer finish, first seal (spray) with sanding sealer. Sand this coat—it will be dry in about half an hour—with 280-grit paper, clean as before, and spray on the first coat of lacquer. If the first or subsequent coats go on without any roughness, you don't need to

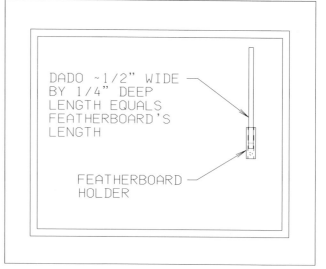

DADO ~1/2" WIDE
BY 1/4" DEEP
LENGTH EQUALS
FEATHERBOARD'S
LENGTH

FEATHERBOARD
HOLDER

FEATHERBOARD HOLDER MOUNTING

sand between coats. The advantage of a lacquer finish is that you can complete the finishing of the station in a couple hours. There is nothing worse than having wet pieces laying all over the place when you want to get on with your work.

Sprayed on lacquer will amalgamate, unlike paint or other coatings that need the surface to be rough-ened for the next coat to adhere. You will probably still be doing some sanding between coats; use a sanding block with 220-grit paper. Three coats of lacquer will be plenty, and your station will be beautiful. It's probably best to scratch it or ding it now so you'll be willing to use it as a workstation.

Drawings, Cutting List and Materials List

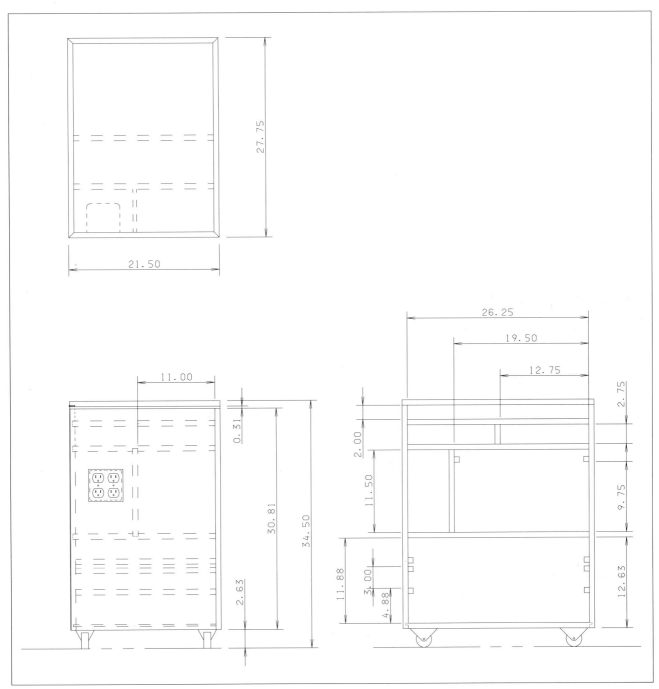

OUTLINE AND DIMENSIONED DRAWINGS

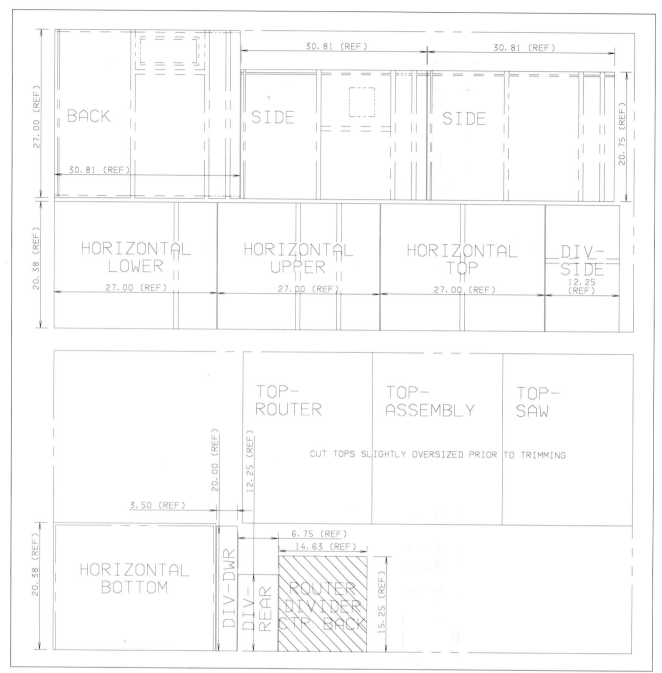

CUTTING DIAGRAM

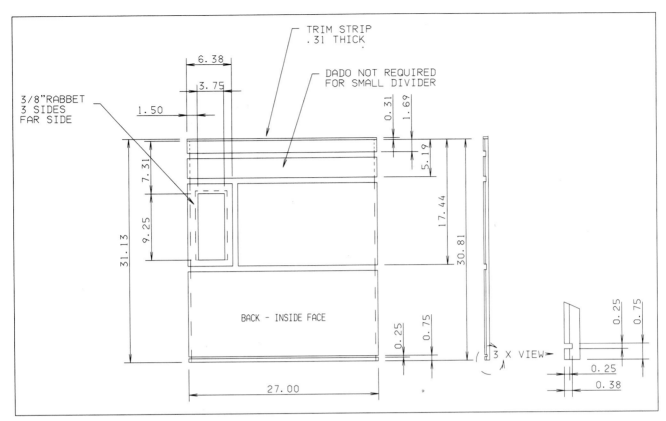

BACK

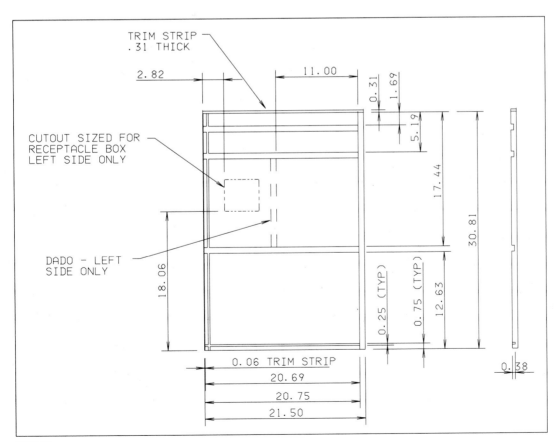

SIDES

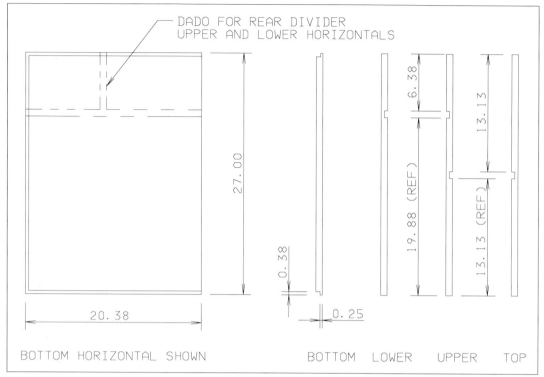

DADO FOR REAR DIVIDER
UPPER AND LOWER HORIZONTALS

27.00

6.38

13.13

19.88 (REF)

13.13 (REF)

0.38

0.25

20.38

BOTTOM HORIZONTAL SHOWN

BOTTOM   LOWER   UPPER   TOP

HORIZONTALS

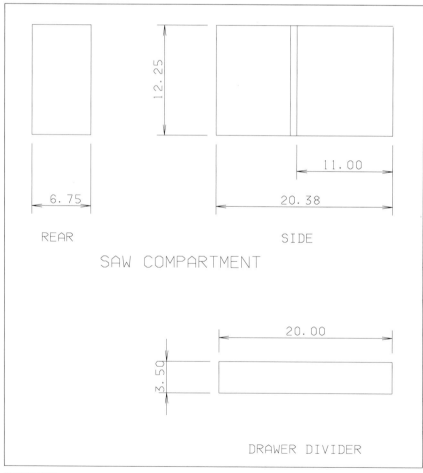

12.25

11.00

6.75

20.38

REAR

SIDE

SAW COMPARTMENT

20.00

3.50

DRAWER DIVIDER

DIVIDERS

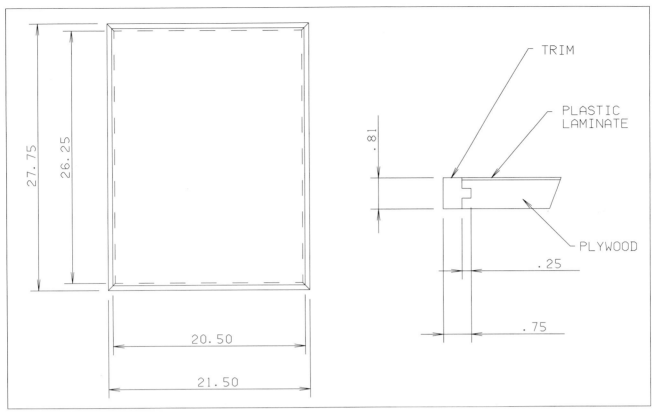

TRIM

PLASTIC
LAMINATE

PLYWOOD

.81

.25

.75

27.75

26.25

20.50

21.50

TOP

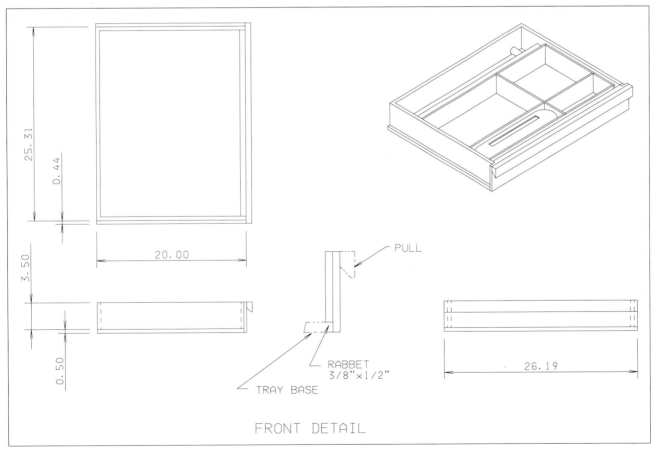

25.31

0.44

3.50

0.50

20.00

PULL

RABBET
3/8"×1/2"

TRAY BASE

26.19

FRONT DETAIL

LOWER TRAY

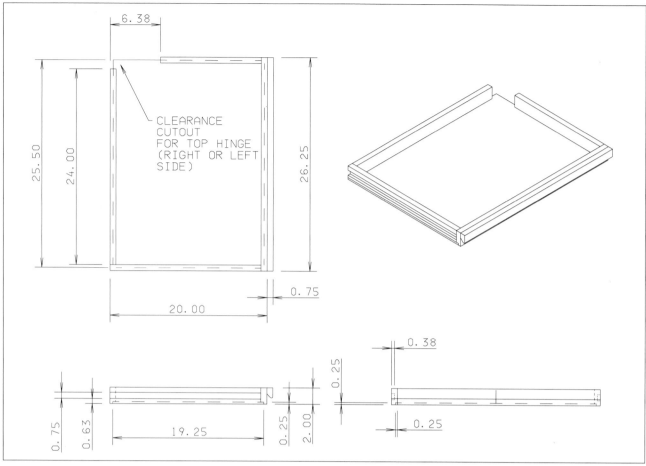

CLEARANCE
CUTOUT
FOR TOP HINGE
(RIGHT OR LEFT
SIDE)

UPPER TRAY

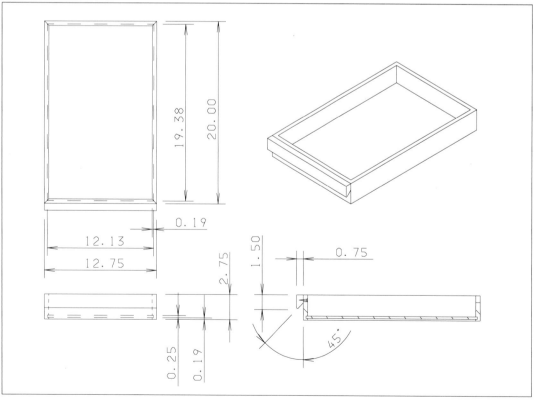

DRAWER

HARDWARE

PART	QTY	DESCRIPTION	SOURCE	COMMENTS
Wheels	4	Casters, 2" swivel		
Lid Support	1	Use the high torque (95–125 inch/lbs.) style.	Woodworker's Supply PN. 100-041	Right or Left. Right PN. 100-040
Hinge	4	Piano Hinge — 1-$\frac{1}{16}$ inch		
Double Gang Receptacle Box	1			
15 amp Double Receptacle	2			Or 1 receptacle and 1 flat switch
4 Outlet Cover Plate	1			
Power Cord	10 ft.	14-gauge, 2 conductor plus ground		
Connector	1	3-prong style		

CUTTING LIST
Carcase—See Cutting Diagram

PART	QTY	DESCRIPTION	MATERIAL	COMMENTS
Back	1	30.81" x 27.00" (30$\frac{13}{16}$" x 27")	¾" Shop Birch	
Side	2	30.81" x 20.75" (30$\frac{13}{16}$" x 20¾")	¾" Shop Birch	Right and Left
Horizontals	4	20.38" x 27.00" (20⅜" x 27")	¾" Shop Birch	Dadoes and cutouts define particular position.
Divider—Side	1	12.25" x 20.38" (12¼" x 20⅜")	¾" Shop Birch	
Divider—Rear	1	6.75" x 12.25" (6¾" x 12¼")	¾" Shop Birch	
Divider—Drawer	1	3.25" x 20.00" (3¼" x 20")	¾" Shop Birch	
Runners	8	¾" x ¾" x required length (cut to fit)	Hardwood	
Tray Supports				
Trim	—	¾" x ¾" border trim. Approximately 3' x 8' Same material will be used for drawer pulls and other trims.	Hardwood	Pick wood color desired—contrasting or blending.

DRAWERS

PART	QTY	DESCRIPTION	MATERIAL	COMMENTS
Top Drawer	2			
Front/Back	4	2.75" x 12.75" (2¾" x 12¾")	½" Baltic birch plywood	
Side	4	2.75" x 20.00" (2¾" x 20")	½" Baltic birch plywood	
Bottom	2	12.38" x 19.50" (12⅜" x 19½")	¼"	MDF, Hardboard or KorTron, etc.
Lower Tray				
Front Face	1	4.00" x 26.19" (4" x 26³⁄₁₆")	½" Baltic birch plywood	
Front/Back	2	3.50" x 25.31" (3½" x 25⁵⁄₁₆")	½" Baltic birch plywood	
Side	2	3.5" x 20.0" (3½" x 20")	½" Baltic birch plywood	
Bottom	1	26.19" x 20.00" (26³⁄₁₆" x 20")	½" Baltic birch plywood	
Upper Tray				
Front/Back	1	2.00" x 26.25" (2" x 26¼")	¾" Baltic birch plywood	Back cut for lid support
Side	4	2" x 20"	¾" Baltic birch plywood	One side requires a cutout for lid support clearance.
Bottom	2	19.25" x 25.50" (19¼" x 25½")	¼" 5 layer plywood	
Drawer Pulls	6	1.5" x 80.0" (1½" x 80")	1" (¾") hardwood	Pick wood color desired—contrasting or blending.

TOP

PART	QTY	DESCRIPTION	MATERIAL	COMMENTS
Base	1	26.75" x 20.50" (26¾" x 20½")	¾" Shop Birch	See section on "Workstation Tops," page 16.
Borders	—	1.5" x 100.0" (1½" x 100")	¾" hardwood	Pick wood color desired—contrasting or blending.
Top Surface	1	26.75" x 20.50" (26¾" x 20½")		See section on "Workstation Tops," page 16.

THE ROUTER WORKSTATION

**THE ROUTER
WORKSTATION**

The router has become one of the most versatile and valuable tools available to the woodworker. Forty years ago the router was a novelty, and even ten years ago it was still a specialty tool. Today, with the tremendous selection in power and bits, there is very little that the router cannot do. For the home or small shop builder the router can replace the jointer, the shaper and even the planer.

The router has recently become a stationary power tool in addition to being a portable power tool. And power it has. Quality router motors now draw from 8 to 15 amps. Many offer "soft start" and variable speed control. To realize the potential of today's routers, you need a platform to build on. That platform is the router workstation.

Router Station Organization

This station, in addition to being a router table, will store most of the tools, bits and accessories that you will be using with your router. It has special wiring that allows switch control of the router motor from either side of the station. As shown in the picture on page 45, it uses the Incra Fence System in addition to special fences that are described here and in chapter six. The design includes storage for a dovetail fixture, a custom design bit storage drawer, and four additional small drawers for bits and the miscellaneous goodies that come with all router accessories. A large drawer at the bottom of the station will hold additional routers and lots more. Your task is to organize all of this paraphernalia so you can get at it, not lose it, and keep it from getting mixed up with the other bits and pieces. This means making more cigar boxes that fit in these drawers.

The router table can be used from either side. For most work the near side—that is, the side where the drawers open—is used. When additional table surface is needed, the far side is used or the other stations are called up in support. The sides of the station can be festooned with all the other things, like C-clamps and fences, that either don't fit in the drawers or that you want to get to quickly. The station may end up looking like a main battle tank outfitted to do battle with all of the world's evil forces. This is appropriate since, when outfitted with hearing protectors, face shield and dust mask, you will look more like a member of the delta force than a woodworker.

The station does not have a miter slot. Instead, a special miter used with the combination fence is provided that is better than a miter slot and easier to use. (For those who feel deprived at not having a miter slot, I've included suggestions on how to add one in the section, "Building the Router Workstation".) There is also a sliding miter fence, which is part of the new, but not replacement, fence system described in chapter six. Collectively, the router workstation and its accessories will allow you to quickly and easily perform just about any router task.

How to use a router is not the subject of this book. If you don't already have one, get one or more of the good books available on this subject. This book describes how to build and use the router station and its special tools, fixtures and jigs.

The following photographs and drawings—each worth at least a thousand words—show how the station has been designed to be used in support of most table routing operations.

Wildcat Kelly of "Don't Fence Me In" fame would not be happy with the number of fences used with the router station. There are fences for standard cuts, jointing, precision cutting, and end cutting of vertical workpieces. Collectively, they should take care of all of your needs.

The combination fence is the primary fence for standard routing operations. One side is used for straight cuts and the other side for jointing. Because it won't fit in the station, this fence is one of the festooned items.

The special miter is used with the combination fence to end-cut stock.

The special miter has two primary advantages over the saw type miter used with many router tables. First, it allows you clamp the workpiece closer to the router bit, providing a stronger clamp that is less likely to slip or chatter. The second advantage is that it rides along the fence, not in a miter slot, and therefore requires no special positioning and adjusting of the fence with respect to the miter.

When used with a bridge fence, the special miter can cut dadoes in small workpieces.

A bridge fence is an elevated fence that allows the

SPECIAL MITER
I recommend the special miter over a saw-type miter. This design rides the fence, and the workpiece is clamped closer to the router cutter bit than it would be with a saw miter. In this picture, the special miter is shown with the miter fence.

workpiece to slide under it. The special miter rides the fence surface. Use this setup when the workpiece is too narrow to use the fence only. An example of a bridge fence is shown at right. The elevators shown are ⅞" blocks.

The vertical miter and miter fence are adaptations of the combination fence and special miter. The miter fence is larger and is used on the far side of the station table only. This fence and miter are designed for large workpieces. You may want to postpone building this set until you need them.

This special miter fits under the router when not in use. (See page 48.)

The fences are stored on the side of the workstation as shown in a number of the pictures. The vertical miter can be stored in the station's bottom drawer; its handle will block the Incra fence but not enough to bother or really get in the way. I keep mine on a shelf since I don't need it that often.

For precision cutting, there is the Incra Fence System or the fence system described in chapter six. Consult the Incra manual on how to use the Incra jig and its accessories.

When not being used, the Incra fence is stored as a drawer. The same runners that hold the Incra jig can be used for storing a dovetail fixture.

To use the dovetail jig, clamp it to the router station top. For that matter, it can be clamped to any of the stations. I normally clamp mine to the sanding and gluing station's extension table. (See page 49.)

The way I store my dovetail fixture breaks the rule of never having to move something to get at the tool or fixture you want. My rationale is this: The dovetail fixture is not used that frequently, and when it is used, it remains in place (out of storage) for considerable periods of time.

Let's not forget the router. When not in use, the router is stored directly under the workstation's top. This allows the station and its top to be used as a regular work surface. There is a special shelf in the router compartment for storing the router attached to its base. If you use a Porter-Cable 690 router, the router motor can be removed and used with other Porter-Cable bases. (See page 49.)

One slot of the router station has been designed to accept a custom drawer for your router bits. This drawer will hold forty ½" and ¼" bits. I use it to store ¼" bits and store my primary ½" bits in a lift-out tray that fits in the small center drawer.

BRIDGE FENCE
Since the special miter does ride the fence, it's necessary to raise the fence when cutting the workpiece anywhere other than at the end. This setup is a bridge fence. The fence is raised by placing simple standoff blocks (elevators) at either end of the fence. The fence shown is a standard style.

VERTICAL MITER AND MITER FENCE
The vertical miter is used only with the miter fence. It offers firm clamping at the cutter while it positions workpieces that must be held in a vertical position. You might use the vertical fence, for example, when using a drawer or lock miter joint bit.

The other drawers should be organized to fit your particular storage needs. Plans for a chest of drawers that fits the bottom drawer opening are included in this book. This chest is very handy because it can be set on another workstation for easy access to its contents.

The Router

The primary router and many of the router accessories described here are from Porter-Cable. I will list the reasons that led me to select the Porter-Cable (P-C) routers, which will at least give you some criteria for router selection, if you don't already own a good one. Note that many of the special attributes of this router workstation take advantage of the feature that allows the P-C motor to be separated from its base.

Criteria for Router Selection

Power. At least 1½ horsepower.

Collet. ¼" and ½" collets. Should be easy to use and easy to change bits. No bit slippage and no locked or frozen cutter shafts!

Design. The P-C design allows the motor unit to be used with three different base units: a D-handle, a plunge and a standard two-handle. This feature is incorporated in the router workstation design but is not a requirement. The Ryobi RE-600 is also used with this design, as is the Dremel Moto-Tool. The station even allows you to mount the Sears Bis-Kit for tabletop plate jointing and a saber saw.

Power Switch. Examine how the router is turned on and off. When using the router as a portable power tool, the D-handle version P-C router, which has a trigger switch, is super. The standard model, on the other hand, leaves something to be desired. What I don't like about the standard model switch is that it is protected from inadvertent turn-on so effectively that it is also hard to turn off. I think a trigger switch of some form is always best for portable applications. For routers that are used with router stations, the on-off switch normally works best. The one disadvantage is that, when used in a table, the motors are normally set to the "on" position. When you take the router out to do portable cutting, it may surprise you when you plug it in.

Depth Adjustment. Depth of cut is height of cut when you are using a router table. Make sure you get the maximum possible. The P-C plunge base allows a

STORING THE SPECIAL MITER
The special miter's base is sized to fit in the router cavity. This is just one example of where arbitrary dimensions are made specific so that the tool fits in the space available. Another example of an arbitrary dimension is the location of the peg that holds the router collet wrenches. If I'd planned ahead, I would've set it 1" higher.

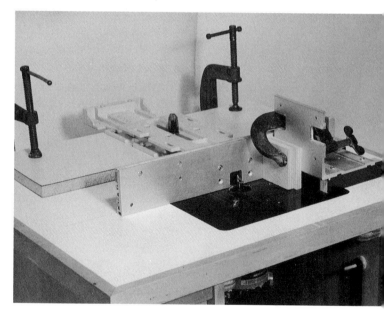

INCRA FENCE
The Incra Fence System offers a wide range of precision cutting features. When not in use, the fence is stored above the station's bottom drawer. Its clamping base is sized to the width of the station opening and slides in like a drawer.

2" plunge. The basic P-C design allows the collet to reach the router table surface.

Bushing Guides. A full set is recommended.

Dovetail Fixture. Nice to have. A must for certain work.

Edge Guide. Also nice to have, but I usually end up using my own homemade guides.

Other Accessories. You may need them someday. Look over what's available.

Other Manufacturers. You can tell which routers are popular by the support given by accessory manufacturers. Pick a router brand that is supported by these specialty manufacturers. Any manufacturer in this business supports Porter-Cable routers. Porter-Cable also offers a very complete selection of accessories for its routers.

I also have a number of other routers, including the Ryobi RE-600 and a Sears Commercial Craftsman that is about 25 years old and still running fine. Some of my routers are dedicated to specific tasks and are only changed when the bits need sharpening.

The good router manufacturers are constantly upgrading the quality and versatility of their products. Read the reviews, pick what meets your needs, and you will probably be happy with your selection for many years. There have been more improvements in the last five years than in the previous 30. But this doesn't mean that your router will become obsolete. Well-designed tools never become obsolete; they become collector's items.

Router Bit Selection

When starting out to do serious work, get a good set of bits. I usually buy a new router bit when I need it. Planning ahead means that I'm ready to make the cut and can't find the proper bit. I have a lot of bits, so normally I can find something that will work. I have even changed designs at this point to make what I wanted fit what bits I have. When I do plan ahead, I will buy a carbide-tipped, ½" shank bit if available. I will also buy P-C or Bosch bits if possible, but in reality I have a very eclectic collection of bits. I buy the ½" shank because I have read that they are safer, and I know that I feel safer using them. I buy P-C bits because they are manufactured for Porter-Cable routers and collets. They also have a new chip-limiting design that eliminates kickback by limiting the amount of material being removed even if the piece is fed too fast into the bit. Another new feature is a black

DOVETAIL JIG

The dovetail jig is stored behind the Incra jig. Its clamping base is also sized to fit the opening. The jig is a little hard to spot in the picture since it's stored upside down with only its base showing. This is done to make the most economical use of the space. The open drawer in the picture gives further evidence of the amount of storage available in this station.

ROUTER STORAGE

The router base, with or without the router motor attached, can be stored under the station top. Stored in this way it's easy to put back in operation. While the router is in storage, the station can be used as another work surface or take-up station.

oxide coating, which keeps resin from accumulating on the bit. I spend a lot of time cleaning bits. This oxide is a real boon to router users.

Building the Router Workstation

The Carcase

All of the carcases are constructed in a similar manner. If you have jumped ahead and are building the router workstation first, go back and read the earlier section on building the table saw workstation.

Cut the pieces from the ¾" birch sheet, mark them, and lay out the cuts to be made. With the router station you must cut the electrical openings at this time. You won't be able to get to them later.

The building sequence is the same as for the table saw station except that a subassembly carcase is glued together first and then, as a completed assembly, is joined (glued) to the remaining parts.

Steps 1 through 5 for the router station are the same as they were for the table saw station.

Step 1. Cut and mark the component pieces.

Step 2. Check the layout.

Step 3. Cut the rabbets.

Step 4. Cut the dadoes.

If you are cutting the dadoes on the saw, remember to cut the corresponding dado in each piece before cutting the next dado (as in the bookcase example). If you are using your router, use the router jig. Cut the openings for the electrical connections. The runners used to support the Incra jig and the dovetail fixture can be done later.

Step 5. Dry assemble and check fit.

As before, sand and clean the pieces before starting to glue up the assemblies.

Step 6. Glue and clamp the subassembly.

Although the back is not glued on at this time, it is a good idea to use it as a pattern to position the fit of the subassembly and particularly to position the edges of the subassembly that will fit into the station's back piece. When the glue has set, assemble the remaining pieces.

1. Place the subassembly onto the back.
2. Position the sides onto the back and the subassembly.
3. Slide in the bottom horizontal.
4. Slide in the router baseplate holder.

CUSTOM BIT STORAGE DRAWER

Access to your router bits is always important. This drawer can hold up to 40 bits, and most importantly, the cutting profiles are discernible for selection. The bars holding the bits rotate back for viewing of the bits and forward for the removal of the selected bit.

ROUTER TABLE SETUP

A newspaper can't get all the news on the front page, and the same is true with all of the tools, fixtures and aids stored in the router workstation. The second and third pages for keeping these tools at your fingertips are the other workstations.

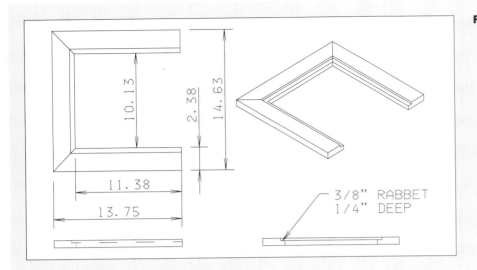

ROUTER HOLDER

3/8" RABBET
1/4" DEEP

MAKING THE ROUTER HOLDER

The router holder fits under the router top and is used for storing the router and the baseplate. Cut the strips from ¾" plywood scrap.

We're getting close now. Cut the ¼" drawer dividers and slide them into their respective dado slots. There is no need to glue these dividers into position since they will be held captive by the trim strips. Not gluing them will also ensure that there will be no glue overflow to worry about.

5. Glue on the trim strips.
   Cut and glue the trim strips and then attach the wheels and the blocks.
6. Attach wheels and blocks.

The lower compartment is designed to hold the 18" Incra fence, a dovetail jig and a drawer. A pair of runners is used to allow these fixtures to slide in above the drawer. The setup described here is for the 18" Incra Fence System and the Sears 12" Dovetail Template.

Both the Incra fence and the Sears dovetail are attached to baseplates that, in turn, are used to clamp the fixtures to the tabletop. These baseplates are cut to a length that allows the fixture to slide into the station as a drawer. For the most economical use of space, turn the dovetail fixture upside down when storing. The dovetail fixture goes in first, which means that you must remove the Incra jig to get at it.

Top

Before starting on the top of the router workstation, review the material in chapter one on building tops. Many of the techniques described in this earlier section will be applied to making the top for the router workstation. The two really important features of the top are these: the top must be a smooth, continuous surface and it must also be a true rectangle. This is complicated by the inclusion of a removable plate as part of the top's surface.

If you have had any experience with router tables, you know that a clamped workpiece will find any obstruction or cranny on the table's surface, and once found, the obstruction will cause the workpiece to stop or jump. It's the Troll of the Top who does this by reaching up and saying, "Gotcha." Trolls don't like smooth, clean surfaces. To ensure that there is no home for a troll and to create this mirrorlike machined surface, you must take some care during the top's construction. Most of the techniques were described earlier in "Workstation Tops." Here we will look at the special needs of the router station top.

Top Construction. The top is composed of a base of dimensionally stable material, such as shop birch, MDF or Baltic birch plywood, covered with Formica, hardboard or some similar surface covering, and framed with a hardwood border. A hole is cut in this top that is sized to accept the router table plate. The cutting list depicts the top being constructed using shop birch. The 14-ply Baltic birch plywood is a preferred material, but it is also more expensive.

Cut the station's top about ½" oversize so that it can

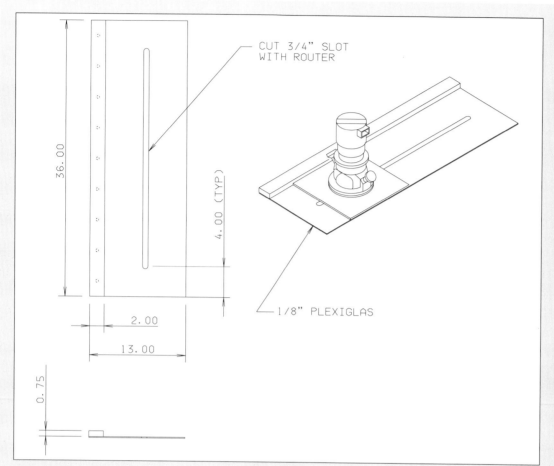

CUT 3/4" SLOT
WITH ROUTER

36.00

4.00 (TYP)

1/8" PLEXIGLAS

2.00

13.00

0.75

ROUTER AND ROUTER GUIDE
The router guide is designed to be used with the router attached to its baseplate. Using a clear base allows you to align the guide with the cut marks easily. The router and guide shown here are being used to cut the dadoes in the table saw workstation.

ROUTER GUIDE

When you use the router for dadoing, a special guide can help make the work easier and more accurate. Normally, one router base is always attached to the router table baseplate. This plate is a very stable platform for routing dadoes and similar cuts when using the router as a portable tool. The solution is a router guide designed to be used with the router attached to its table baseplate. This guide is shown here.

CONSTRUCTION OF THE ROUTER GUIDE

You can construct the guide easily and quickly. Screw a 2" x 36" dressed strip of ¾" hardwood or good plywood stock to a piece of ⅛" polycarbonate cut to 13" x 36". Then use a router with a ¾" bit to cut the slot. To use the guide to cut a ¾" dado, align the left edge of the slot with the left edge of the desired dado as marked on the workpiece, then clamp it in place and make the dado cut.

be cut to its exact dimensions after the laminate has been bonded to it (see chapter one). Cut the laminate slightly larger than the oversized top dimensions, and then bond the laminate to the top using contact cement. As always, use a good quality contact cement. When cutting the top you can also cut and cover the plate that will be used to fill the hole in the top. This cover plate makes a good template for making the router table plate.

Cut the top to 26.25" x 20.00". Now comes the fun part. You want to cut a square hole into the top that is exactly ¾" less than the size of the chosen baseplate. If you are making your own baseplate, cut the hole to the planned dimensions, and then cut the baseplate(s) to fit this hole. This is an easier sequence. You can also plan for some slight trimming of the baseplate. You want to end up with a good fit. If you will be using multiple baseplates, they must all be the same size; the hole in the top is the master pattern. You will want to be able to use multiple baseplates.

Start by cutting the hole undersized with a saber saw, and then trim the edges to the required opening using a pattern bit in your router. The pattern for the pattern bit is made from ½" or ¾" strips, depending on the cutting length of the bit you are using. These strips are tacked or nailed to the bottom side of the top, with the edges of the strips on the cutting line. This method will allow you to cut a good, clean opening.

When using the router like this, do two things: (1) Use wide strips to give support for the router base, and (2) tape a block of wood to the router base that is of the same stock as the pattern. This will ensure that your cut is perpendicular to the top's surface by keeping the router from wobbling. You will also have to put the cutout piece from the top back in the hole to give the router and block a surface to ride on. If you use a router pad, the various pieces won't move when you are making the trim cuts. Use the saw's cutoff jig to trim the cutout piece down to a size that will offer support but not get in the way of the router bit. This whole setup will have to be elevated enough to allow the router bit to make the cut in the workstation top and not in the top of your bench surface.

The ⅜" rabbet can be cut now or later, after the border trim has been installed. In cutting this rabbet, rout your way into the final depth of the cut with successive passes and adjustments of the depth of cut. If you do go too far, some plate manufacturers have suggested the use of thumbtacks. I have used duct tape for shimming. I cut thin strips of the tape and then placed them on the ledge of the rabbet. If the baseplates aren't the same thickness—if, for example, you are using phenolic, polycarbonate or plywood—then you must shim the thinner material until it is the same thickness as the thicker piece. Unfortunately, ¼" plastics are sometimes .250" thick and sometimes 6mm thick (.236"). I now make all of my plates from either ¾" 14-layer Baltic birch plywood or a glue-up of ¼" and ½" or two ⅜" plates of Baltic birch plywood. If I need to shim I use wood edging tape. This is the same tape used to cover exposed plywood edges and is put

USING THE PATTERN CUTTER

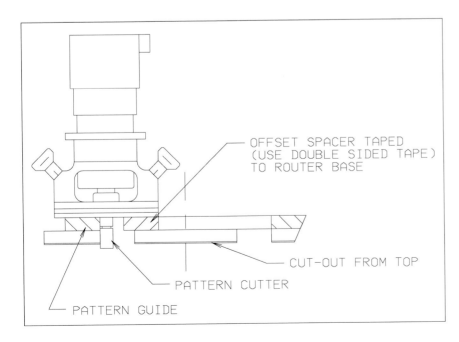

OFFSET SPACER TAPED
(USE DOUBLE SIDED TAPE)
TO ROUTER BASE

CUT-OUT FROM TOP

PATTERN CUTTER

PATTERN GUIDE

on with an iron. The ⅟₆₄" tape can be sanded or doubled up if needed.

To complete the top, the border trim is glued on, and a plate is made to fill the router baseplate hole when the router is not being used. Dowels are used to strengthen the border-to-top mounting. You can also use biscuits. The Dowel Pro is a good jig when you are using dowels and for most other doweling applications. Plan to leave not more than ⅟₃₂" overhang of the border trim for subsequent trimming. To get the required overhang you will need a shim of some sort to fool the doweling jig, which is manufactured to create a flush surface. The problem is that sometimes that fit is not flush. You can use two or three business cards for this shimming; the number will depend on how much you or your company spends on the business cards. Thin cards are normally cheaper than thick cards.

The best way to attach the top to the carcase is with screws. You will notice that there are few places you can get at to attach the top. Use the electrical opening in the back and the router cavity in the front to drill the pilot holes for the attachment screws. Four No. 10 screws will be plenty.

The plate used to fill the baseplate hole can be cut from either ¼" stock or from ¾" stock. The ¼" plate fits the opening just like a polycarbonate or phenolic router baseplate. If you use ¾" stock, then it will be necessary to rabbet the edges to fit the opening. The two styles are shown here. I have been making the plates from the ¾" plywood stock. If I need a new router plate, I steal the cover plate.

I prefer the ¾" rabbeted plate because it stays in place better and can be used as a template. Surface the plate with the laminate used for the top.

The first router plate used in this design came from Oak Park, Ltd. Oak Park formerly supplied baseplates for most routers and a number of supporting accessories for router tables. The advantage in buying a manufactured plate is the ability to buy accessories like inserts that can tax the manufacturing capabilities found in the small shop.

Having said that, I suggest you start by building your own baseplates. Then, if you are going to be using multiple routers and therefore multiple baseplates, you'll know that you're covered and won't have worry about your source of supply. The Baltic birch plywood works well for these plates. Making your own plate from polycarbonate or phenolic sheet is also a good solution, except that the material thickness varies from one lot and one supplier to another, and your plate may require shimming.

If you, like me, own a Ryobi RE-600 router, making your own baseplate is a good idea. Many commercial baseplates for the RE-600 unfortunately do not use the mounting holes recommended by Ryobi for mounting the plate. This router has special tapped holes for use with table router plates. These holes are tapped for an 8mm screw that gives the strength necessary to hold a heavy router. Some commercial designs I've seen use the mounting hole layout for the router's baseplate, which uses a 4mm screw (.315" vs. .157").

To make a baseplate, first cut the blank to the size of the table opening. The blank can be ¾" material, or you can two-step the process by using ¼" stock for the primary plate and then glue on a piece of ½" stock for the subplate. If you have opted to use the ¼" polycarbonate or phenolic, you won't require the subplate. Before rounding the plate's corners, pencil the diagonals onto the blank to locate its center and then center punch that position.

Round the corners and check the fit, trimming as required. If you have the required fit with your cover plate, this plate can be used as the pattern to follow with your pattern bit mounted in the router. Next, place a V-bit in the router and remove the router's baseplate. Place the router on the blank and, using the V-bit, position the router on the blank with the V-bit in the punched center. Mark the mounting hole centers on the blank using the router's subbase as the template. Copy the method used for the router's baseplate attachment when you attach the new baseplate, that is, by counterbore or countersink mounting.

Now drill out the center opening. You may want to step drill so that inserts can be added. For the first baseplate use a 1½" to 2" hole. Some bits that you will be using will require a larger opening. Many of these large bits should not be used at speeds of greater than 10,000 rpm. Use large multispeed routers like the Porter-Cable Speedmatic 7539 or the Ryobi RE-600 with their own baseplate(s).

Attach the new baseplate. Then, letting the V-bit just barely touch the work surface and working with the router guide described earlier, cut trace lines on a piece of wood with each of the four edges and measure the offsets. These measured offsets should then be marked on the new baseplate. (See also the section

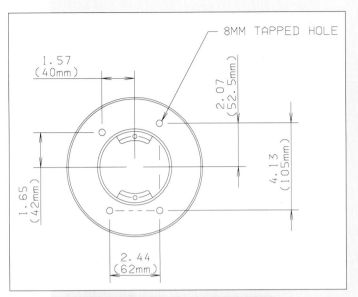

RYOBI R-600 AND RE-600 MOUNTING

RYOBI

Ryobi America Corp. supplied the above information for mounting the R-600 and the RE-600.

With these mounting data, Ryobi noted that the Underwriter's Laboratory implements ANSI standards relative to a shaper for a router used in an inverted table mount application. These rules require proper fences, safety guarding, and an on-off switch supplied from the router. I believe the router workstation meets these standards.

"Corner Jig" on page 72, before trimming the new baseplate.)

The previous instructions assume that you have ended up making an asymmetrical plate. If you were right on the money with the layout and mounting of the router, there won't be any offsets to measure. Although not mandatory, it can be beneficial if the router-to-plate mounting is not perfectly centered. The ideal plate is shown at right.

Considering the left edge the reference edge, the top edge is increased $\frac{1}{64}$", the right edge $\frac{1}{32}$" and the bottom edge $\frac{3}{64}$". Starting with a nominal 11" square, the reference edge of this plate, is cut back $\frac{3}{64}$", the top $\frac{1}{32}$" and the right side $\frac{1}{64}$".

When the router, together with its baseplate, is used with a left side guide, the first cut is made with the reference edge against the fence. Making a second pass with the top edge against the fence will increase the width of the cut by $\frac{1}{64}$". Using the right side will

increase the width of the cut by $\frac{1}{32}$" and so forth. Since base, top right and bottom lose their positional meaning as the base is turned, the sides are marked 0, 1, 2 and 3 respectively, mnemonics for $\frac{0}{64}$", $\frac{1}{64}$", etc.

The reason is that the width of the dado cut by the router bit is the diameter of the bit. Often the width of the material you want to place in the dado is the same or slightly wider. By making a controlled second pass using one of the oversized edges, you can get the exact width dado required.

Now that you have read the engineering solution, you can forget about most of it. Few of us have the tools and fixtures to hold the tolerances discussed. In reality, just remounting the baseplate will change the dimensional relationships of the sides to the edges. The important thing is that you know what the relationships are and recognize that they change if you change the base.

If you want a miter slot for a saw-type miter gauge, double the trim at the top's front edge. Then cut a dado in the center of this 1½" wide trim to accept the miter bar. Don't do this until you have used the station with its special miter and its sliding miter fence.

You're almost there—just a couple more holders, a switch cover plate, the wiring and the drawers. The holders are for the cover plate when it is not being used. There's also a peg to hold the collet wrench(es).

Plate Holder

The cover plate holder fits on the left side of the router cavity. As you can see in the drawing on page 56, the holder is 1" wide. This width, which is accomplished by using some ¼" shim stock with the ¾" stock, allows a slight offset from the side, so that your fingers can get hold of the plate when you want to take it out.

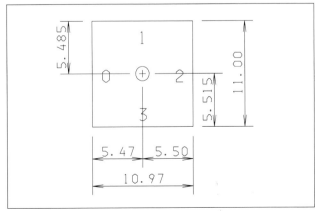

ASYMMETRICAL BASEPLATE—ROUTER WORKSTATION

Switch Plate Cover

The front switch plate is shop made to fit the opening in the carcase. Cut a ¼" piece of plywood to fit the opening and then, using your router, cut away from the back enough material so that the switch can be mounted. Copy the style of a normal receptacle cover plate used in household wiring.

Collet Wrench Peg

If the collet nut wrenches have holes in their handles, they can hang on the right side of the router cavity. This mounting is shown here. A spacer was used to strengthen the peg and to hold the wrenches away from the case side. If you don't have holes in your wrenches, use a strong magnet (Master Magnetics, Inc. Part Number 07001) and add a ledge for the wrench to rest on and to hold it in place.

Wiring the Router Station

Powering the router workstation is accomplished by plugging an extension cord into the wiring box, which is behind the wiring access door on the back of the station. A male base receptacle is used to connect the extension cord to the station. This box also serves as the primary electrical junction box for the station. It ensures that all wiring is covered and can only be accessed by removing the box cover.

Follow the schematic shown here for the actual wiring connections. On-off power to the router is

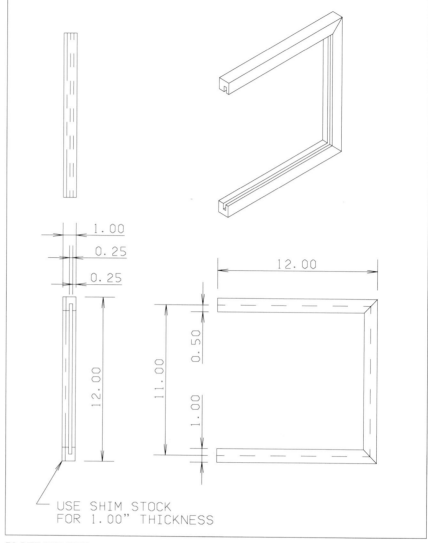

PLATE HOLDER

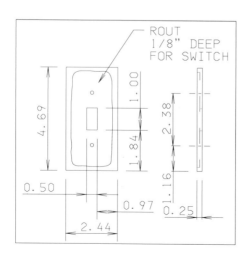

SWITCH PLATE

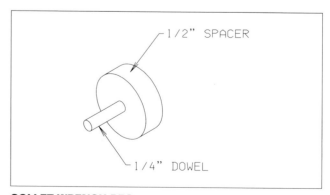

COLLET WRENCH PEG

controlled through either of the two 3-position switches located at the front and back of the station. This allows the station to be used from either side. If you're not used to wiring household circuits, have someone who is check your work. It is a good idea to have the circuit wired in an exposed configuration and checked before buttoning everything up. Doing this will ensure that there is enough slack in the wiring to make changes or repairs.

Remember, there are no grounding provisions in a wooden workstation. It is therefore mandatory that a grounded circuit be used to bring power to the station. For the wiring inside the station, make sure that the ground circuit is completed by wiring the ground wire to all of the receptacles.

The wiring box is a purchased, double-depth receptacle box together with a Sylvania or Bryant connector and a shop-made cover. To locate the mounting holes in this shop-made cover, draw a diagonal from one corner of the cover to the opposite corner, locate the center and then measure from the center back along the diagonal one half of the center-to-center distance between the mounting holes on the receptacle box. This method of layout will give an exact hole location. See the following example.

Drawers

The small drawers on the left side of the router station are made using the "Other Joint." (See illustration on page 58.) This joint is used to maximize the storage capacity of the drawers. Measure the openings and cut to fit. The opening below the switch on the right side houses the custom router bit storage drawer. The plans here show the drawer laid out for ¼" bits.

Examples of how you can make a collection of cigar boxes and trays to fit the left-hand drawers are shown on page 58. I use the cutter tray for ½" bits. The lift handle in the center of the tray is a dowel with a wooden ball.

The lower drawer can be built as a chest of drawers. This is a handy configuration, since the chest can

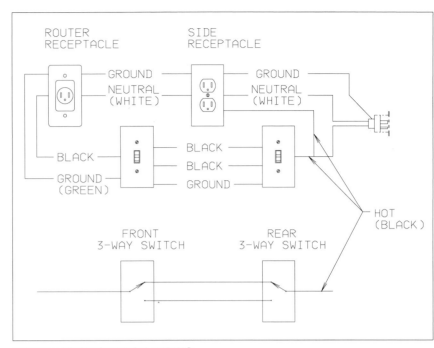

ROUTER WORKSTATION WIRING

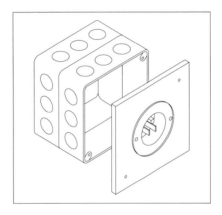

ROUTER WORK-STATION WIRING BOX

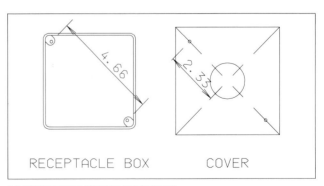

LAYOUT FOR HOLE LOCATION

be pulled out and set on one of the other workstations when you are using your router station.

When making these boxes, remember that if you are using your router, you will forever be buying some new bit or gizmo. Plan for growth and flexibility.

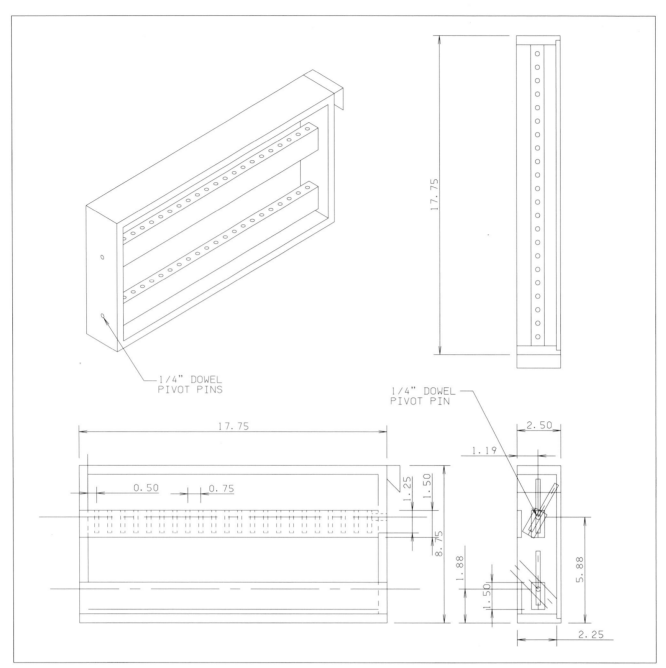

17.75

1/4" DOWEL
PIVOT PINS

1/4" DOWEL
PIVOT PIN

17.75

0.50   0.75

1.25
1.50
1.50
8.75
1.88
1.50

2.50
1.19
5.88
2.25

DRAWERS

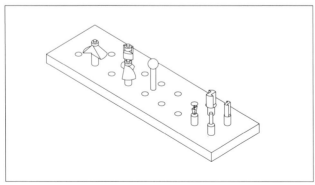

CUTTER TRAY

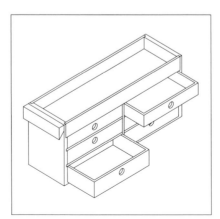

CHEST

Router Workstation Fixtures

As with the table saw workstation, the router workstation has its own work unique fixtures and accessories. Most important of these fixtures are the router fences, which will be used for most routing operations.

It is said that good fences make good neighbors. With router tables, good fences make good cuts. The type of cut determines the type of fence you need. In the beginning, the fence you'll use most frequently will probably be the straight or normal side of the combination straight and jointer fence. Later, you will probably be using the sliding miter fence, described in chapter six, the most.

Instead of making the cutout for the largest router bit you will ever need, make multiple fences with the hole sized for classes of bits, e.g., small, medium and large. You want as much fence support around the cutter bit as possible.

Combination Straight and Jointer Fence

Since the router placement in the router workstation is asymmetrical, a simple fence can be used as a straight fence and as a jointer fence. This combi-

nation fence is shown below.

Note that the fence is offset on one side. This offset is the jointing cut dimension.

Making the Combination Fence. The fence is made so that there are two fence surfaces to work with: one for jointer cutting and one for normal edge cutting. To make the fence, first cut four ¾" plywood strips about 3" wide, and then glue them together as two sets of two strips each. Make the 45° cuts in one pair, and cut the router bit clearance holes and the clamping slots in the other pair. When gluing what will be the bottom strips together, make sure that one edge is slightly offset with respect to the edge of the other strip. After you've made the required cuts, glue the two pairs together as shown in the example on page 60.

When making this glue-up, make sure that the offset plywood edge protrudes beyond the other strips' edges. This is done so that there is a continuous edge that can ride against the saw's fence when the glued-up block is being trimmed.

After the glue has set, trim the fence to the suggested 2" width. As always, make sure you have a square, flat piece when finished.

Having completed the basic fence, set your rip

COMBINATION FENCE

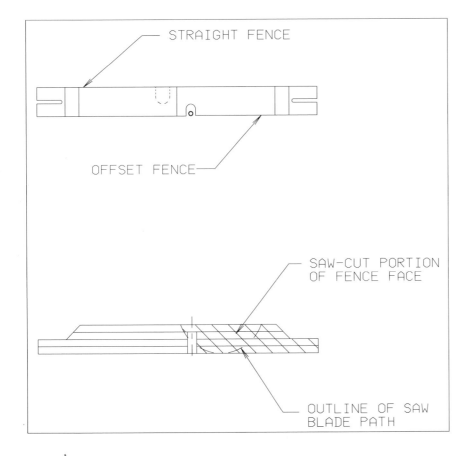

STRAIGHT FENCE

OFFSET FENCE

SAW-CUT PORTION OF FENCE FACE

OUTLINE OF SAW BLADE PATH

fence on the table to not more than $\frac{1}{16}$" less than the router fence's finished width. Place the combination fence upside down on the table saw, and cut the offset up to the router bit opening. This is now the jointer side of the fence.

Using the Jointer Fence Side. For clarity, the picture here is an exaggerated representation of the offset in the fence and the fence's relationship to the router cutter bit. This relationship is established by the cutter's guide bearing. A flush-cutting pattern bit is used for this operation. These bits come with the guide-bearing roller either at the top of the cutter or at the bottom. Either bit can be used.

Align the fence by placing a straightedge against the fence and then positioning the fence and the straightedge against the guide bearing. The fence can now be clamped and is ready for making the jointer cut. If you are using a pattern bit with the bearing next to the router collet, the bit must be lowered below the router table surface after alignment and before joining the workpiece. Either bit will require a cutting length that is greater than the thickness of the stock being joined. Don't try to join surfaces greater than $\frac{3}{4}$".

Use your saw to edge the board to which you want to jointer-surface to the finished width plus $\frac{1}{16}$". Then make the final finishing cut on the router table.

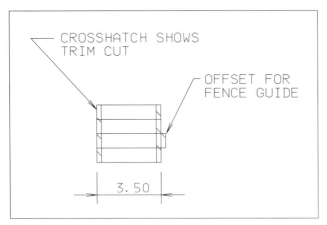

GLUING AND TRIMMING THE COMBINATION FENCE

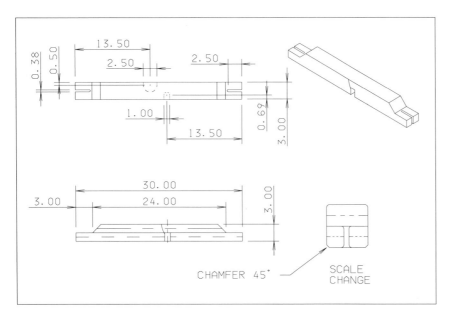

**COMBINATION FENCE—
DIMENSIONED DRAWING**

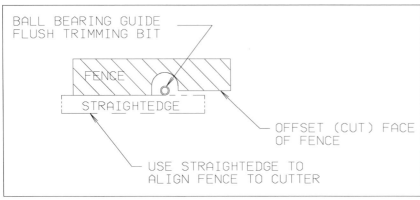

JOINTER TRIMMING

Using the Straight Fence Side. When you use the straight side, the combination fence is like any router fence. Use blocks to raise the fence, making it a bridge fence used in conjunction with the special miter.

The Special Miter

The special miter replaces the saw miter used with many router tables. The special miter offers a number of advantages over the saw-type miter. Most importantly, it is designed for the router, not for the saw. The special miter consists of a block that rides against the router fence, its own fence for positioning the workpiece and a clamp, together with a clamping plate, to hold the workpiece.

The base and block of the special miter are made from ¾" 14-layer plywood. Cut the block strips slightly oversized (about 2½") and glue them together the way you did the combination fence. Trim this glued-up block on one side, and round-over the top edge. Now glue the block with the trimmed side onto the fence base. This fence base should be also cut slightly oversized so that the complete assembly can be trimmed square after the glue has set. The block side, which will run against the router fence, must be exactly 90° to the fence base front.

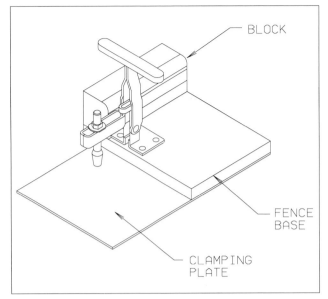

THE SPECIAL MITER

The clamping plate, made from a ⅛" or thicker sheet of Lexan, is bonded to the bottom of the fence base with contact cement and further held with a few No. 4 flathead screws. The quick-release toggle clamp used in this design is the one carried by Woodworker's Supply under their Part No. 812-304.

**THE SPECIAL MITER—
DIMENSIONED DRAWING**

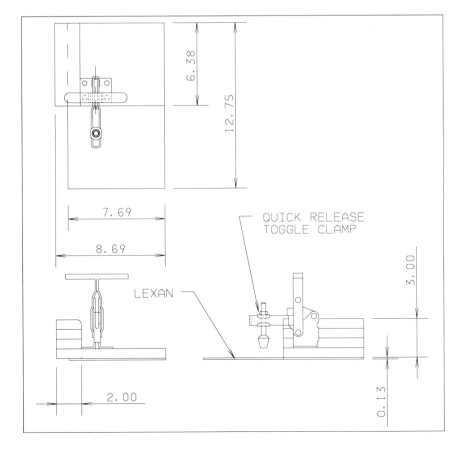

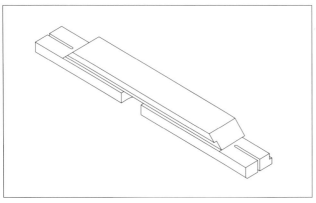

VERTICAL MITER FENCE

Using the Special Miter. Since the special miter rides against the router fence, it is not necessary to align the fence to a miter slot as you would with a saw-type miter. Merely set the fence with respect to the cutter. Clamp the workpiece in the special miter, and keeping the block against the router fence, slide along the fence to make the cut.

The Router Vertical Miter Fence

I developed this fence for the router workstation to handle large stock—for example, cutting the rails and stiles for doors and making vertical end cuts with the special miter gauge.

Making the Router Vertical Miter Fence. The router fence is made from strips of plywood sheet that are glued together. Like the combination fence, these strips are cut oversized and later trimmed using the saw. It is a rather massive fence, designed to support the router's vertical miter attachment and other accessory fixtures. You'll find the construction is straightforward, but make sure the required orthogonality—squareness—is maintained.

The final width of the fence is 4", so cut the strips about 4½" wide to allow the necessary leeway for gluing and clamping. Glue the strips in pairs, forming a bottom half and a top half. With the bottom half, before gluing, first dress one strip to about 4¼" wide. You'll use this board as the reference for the final trimming to the required width. Make sure that the edges of this board are parallel. If need be, tack a straightedge to this strip, then, with this straightedge against the fence, remove the straightedge, turn the board, and cut to the 4¼" width. You now have a board with

ROUTER VERTICAL MITER— DIMENSIONED DRAWING

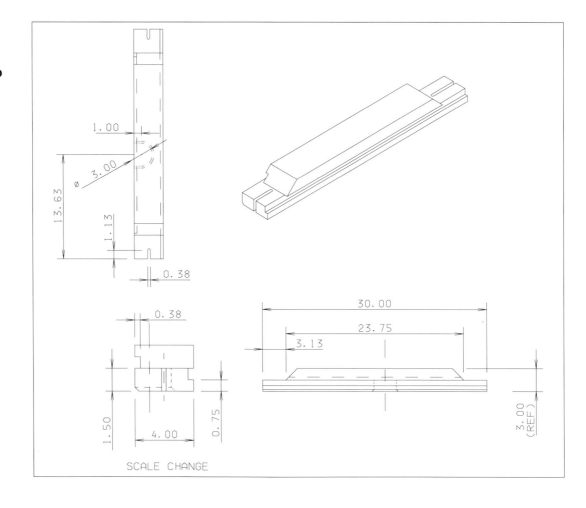

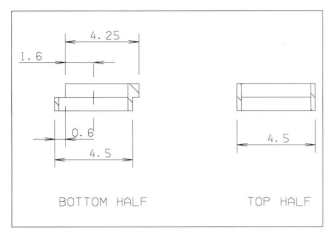

OFFSET EDGE

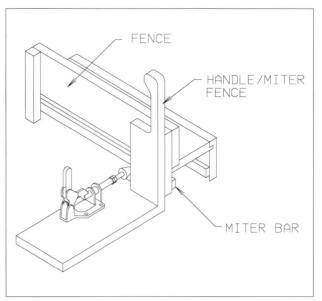

VERTICAL MITER

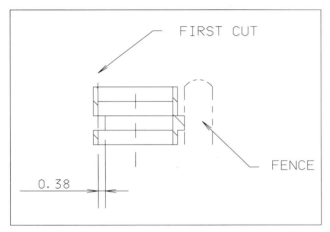

TRIMMING THE FENCE

parallel sides 4¼". I have an old plastic drafting table straightedge (a T square without the T) that works well for this application. You can use this same method to cut the fence to its final width, except that the previously dressed board will replace the straightedge. When you glue the two bottom pieces together, glue the strip that was trimmed so that its sides are offset with respect to the other piece, as shown at the top of the page.

Note that the board with the exposed edge is also offset on the other side, which will result in a dado when the fence is finished. This dado will be used as the miter slot for the router miter. It's because of the router miter that we are going to all this trouble with the fence.

Before you glue the upper and lower halves together, cut the slots for the clamps and cut out the router bit clearance hole. On the top half, if you want the 45° chamfers, cut them now. They should give your hand a little more room when clamping the fence and keep your knuckles from getting too skinned up.

After gluing the top and bottom halves together, you are ready to trim the fence to its final width. Note: As shown in the figure at left, the fence and cut are set to leave a ⅜"-deep slot or dado. This dado can be dressed up later, so don't worry too much about being exactly on the mark.

Make the first cut as shown, with the edge of the previously dressed board riding against the fence. Now turn the board over and cut to the 4" width.

A cleat and knob are used to clamp the fence to the router tabletop when it is not possible to use a C-clamp. (See the sidebar on "Fixture Knobs and Fence Clamps.") The cleat positions under the top's hardwood edge.

Vertical Miter

Conceptually, the vertical miter is similar to a saw miter turned 90°. Think of the router vertical miter fence with its miter slot as the table surface of a table saw. The router bit replaces the saw blade in this analogy. As designed, the vertical miter can hold workpieces up 11" wide. The workpiece is positioned against both the fence and the handle/miter fence and then clamped against the miter bar using the horizontal quick-release clamp. The workpiece can and should be clamped to the fence using C-clamps.

Many of the edge-forming cuts made using the vertical miter are complementary cuts. When using a lock miter cutter or a drawer joint bit, one cut is made with the workpiece held horizontally, and the mating piece is cut while held in the vertical position. Since

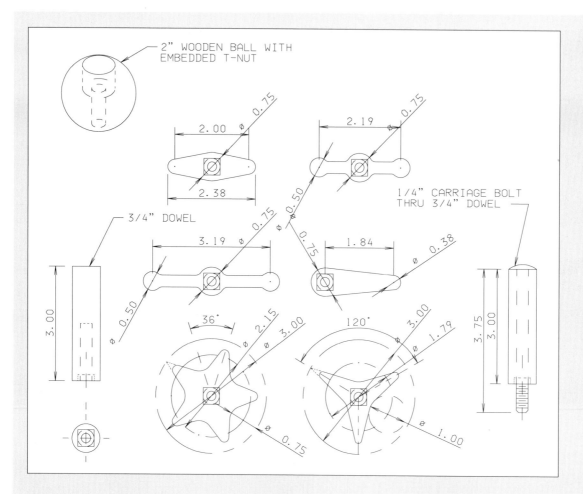

FIXTURE KNOBS AND FENCE CLAMPS

A number of knob styles are used with the jigs and fixtures described throughout the book. Here are some of the basic patterns used. You can change, enlarge upon or ignore these patterns depending on your needs.

For the threaded insert, the simplest solution is to set and epoxy a recessed square nut into the knob or handle. Hexagonal nuts can also be used, but they don't have a wide flat side that resists rotation. On the other hand, if you drill a hole slightly smaller than the nut, it is easier to recess into the wood handle. Other options, such as T-nuts, brass threaded inserts and tapping the wood, all succeed to varying degrees. A lot depends on what you have and how the knob will be used. The same thing applies to the material used for the knobs. Use what you have. If you are buying knobs, you may want to consider the inserts manufactured by Midwest Fastener Corporation. The Midwest Fastener wood insert uses a hex drive, as opposed to a screwdriver slot,

for installation. The hex drive is much easier to install. Midwest also distributes a very large range of specialty hardware, metal and plastic, that can be adapted for many jig applications.

When you cut the knobs, start by drilling the holes that will end up being the concave arcs. A saber saw or band saw can then be used to cut out the individual arms. A handle similar to the locking handle used with the taper jig can hold the knob safely when you do the round-over cutting on the router workstation.

The clamps that hold the fence to the table are made with wooden cleats, bolts, T-nuts or inserts and some form of locking handle.

The cleats are made in a shape that picks up the ledge of the router top. The ball clamp handle, though nice to use, is too large to allow the vertical miter to slide onto the fence when it is clamped to the table. This is the reason for the lower profile, wooden-wheel clamping handles. You can use C-clamps to hold the fences except for the Vertical

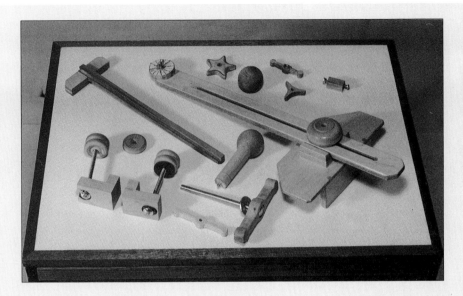

KNOB STYLES
Here is a collection of knobs, cleats and other fixtures used with the jigs described throughout the book. The advantage in making your own knobs is that they are the size you need. You won't save money building your own knobs, but you will have fun making them.

CLEAT

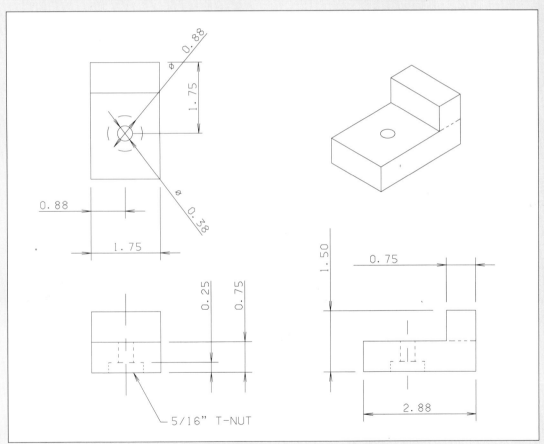

Miter application. I hang my C-clamps on the side of the station.

A ⁵⁄₁₆" carriage bolt connects the cleat to the handle. Fender washers are used under the clamping handles.

VERTICAL MITER—DIMENSIONED DRAWING

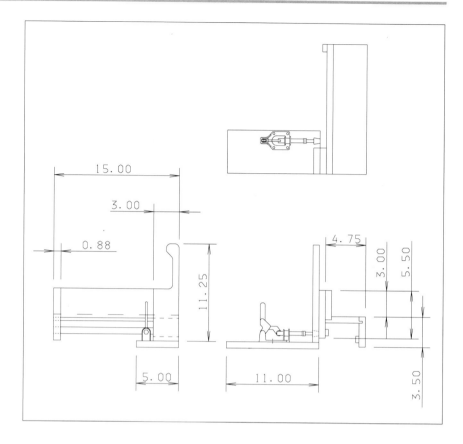

PUSH BLOCKS AND RELATED HOLDING FIXTURES

Here are some examples of the type of push blocks that can be made. The choice of which block to use is determined by the type of cut being made. Also shown is a shop-made foot switch. With many cutting operations, both hands are occupied holding the workpiece. You can use your foot to control the power to the router.

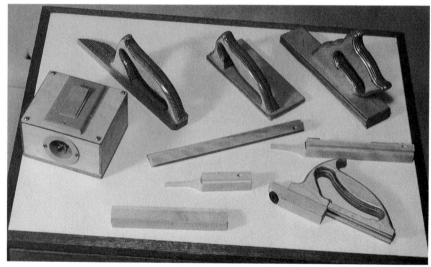

the special miter holds the workpiece above the actual router table surface by the thickness of the clamping plate, it is necessary to clamp the complementary vertical workpiece this same distance off the table surface. The easiest way to do this is to have a strip of the material used for the special miter's clamping plate available as a spacer to hold the workpiece up when it is being clamped in position to the vertical miter. Don't allow the workpiece to drag the spacer into the router bit.

Building the Vertical Miter The vertical miter is a box that rides on the vertical fence. The basic box is made using Baltic birch plywood or MDF. The handle/miter fence, miter bars and the clamp base are made from Baltic birch plywood. For the right-angle connection of the clamp base to the handle, use either a box joint or dovetails. The finished assembly should slide easily without rocking on the vertical miter fence. To keep the miter bar against the vertical miter fence, a strip of hardwood is attached at the end. This strip limits the width of the workpiece. The clamp I've used is the quick-release horizontal carried by

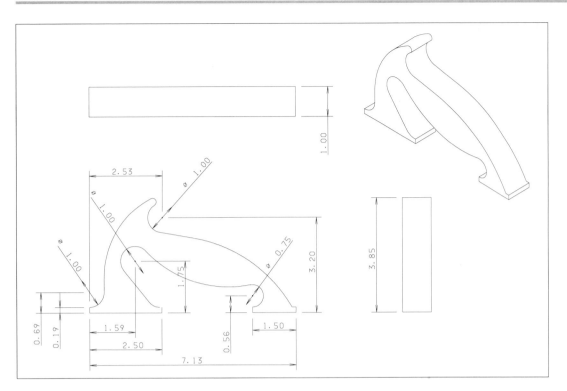

PUSH BLOCK— BASIC PATTERN

PUSH BLOCK SAW-TYPE HANDLE

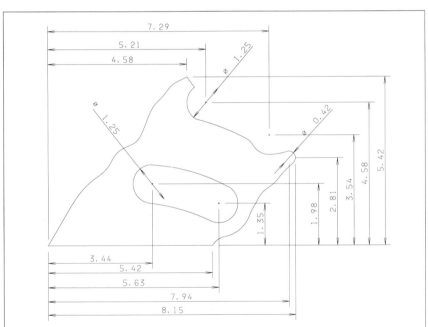

Woodworker's Supply under their Part No. 173-005.

You will need a number of push blocks and related aids when using your router table. Some of them can be purchased. All of them can be made.

Building the Push Blocks. Making your own set of blocks is fun. Shown on page 66 are the ones that I use and how I use them.

To get a 1" thick handle, glue up some scrap Baltic birch plywood, using ¼", ½" or ¾" stock, and cut the handle shapes shown.

This is the basic push block shape used with most of the designs. The saw-type handle is also a good shape to work with. As you can see in the photograph, I use both types.

Plates covered with router pad or some other non-skid material can be attached to a handle to make a push block. Before attaching the handles to the base, use a ⅜" or ½" round-over bit on the handle to make it comfortable. The pad is bonded to the plywood base with 3-M Super 77 spray adhesive.

MAKING SAFE CUTS

Making safe cuts is a matter of using the correct setup. Shown here are two push I handles use frequently. One is a handheld featherboard; the other is a hold-down handle with interchangeable shoes or bases. The handles are large enough to keep the hands away from the cutter bit even if you slip.

SAFETY

There are no guards or other shields for the fences and other fixtures used with the router workstation. My experience has shown that most of these "safety" devices often get in the way of making safe cuts. Remember, if you can get the workpiece to the cutter, it is also possible to get your fingers to the cutter.

If you don't feel comfortable making a cut, the chances are it's not a safe cut and you shouldn't make it. Work from large stock, and make the holder or fixture so that it keeps your hands positioned safely away from the cutter.

The way to make safe cuts is to use the proper setup and use fixture part holders that are designed properly. Build the push blocks and related designs shown here so you can make safe cuts. The push block handles are designed so that, even if the block slips, your hand is kept away from the cutter.

The plate can be a simple rectangular shape as shown at right.

Another shape that is useful both at the router table and the saw is a featherboard base. The push block featherboard is held and used just as you would use a normal featherboard clamped to the station.

By adding a base to the handle, you can make the push handle accept a variety of shapes for holding the workpiece. Because these shapes, called shoes, wear over time, they are removable and separate from the handle. This design allows just about any shape to be used as a push block or hold-down. Shown on page 69 is a short shoe that exerts pressure on the workpiece like a thumb and forefinger would. Cut a reasonable length of the basic shoe stock (i.e., sliding dovetail) and then cut the individual shoes from this stock as needed.

The push block handle is extended by adding a base, which holds the shoe. The interior portion can be cut out using a jig or saber saw, or you can cut

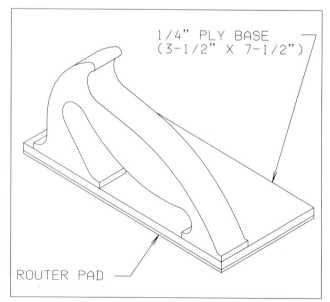

1/4" PLY BASE
(3-1/2" X 7-1/2")

ROUTER PAD

BASIC PUSH BLOCK

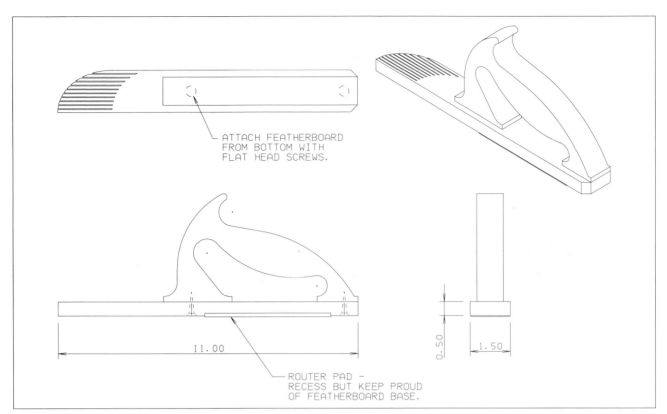

ATTACH FEATHERBOARD
FROM BOTTOM WITH
FLAT HEAD SCREWS.

11.00

ROUTER PAD –
RECESS BUT KEEP PROUD
OF FEATHERBOARD BASE.

0.50   1.50

PUSH BLOCK FEATHERBOARD

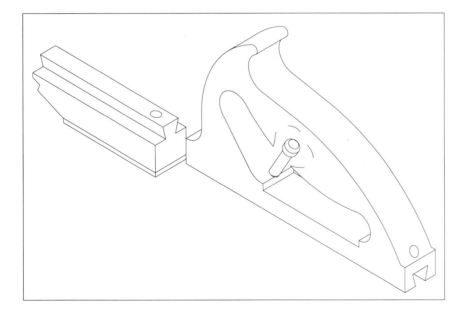

PUSH BLOCK WITH REMOVABLE SHOES

through the base with a band saw. The handle will still be strong and safe.

Use ⁷⁄₃₂" axle pegs to pin the shoes to the handle. To drill the holes for the peg in the handle, slide a piece of shoe stock into the handle and then match drill the rear hole through the handle and the shoe. Next, slide the shoe stock forward so the hole is under the front part of the handle. Using the hole in the shoe as a template, drill the front hole. If you are careful, the two holes will be at the same angle to the base. The hole for shoes that use the front hole for pinning can be drilled using the handle's rear hole as the drill guide. Some handy shapes are shown on the next page.

The picture at the top of page 71 is upside down to show the mounting of the slip gasket. This gasket, which is analogous to your thumb, is easier to replace when it gets too cut up.

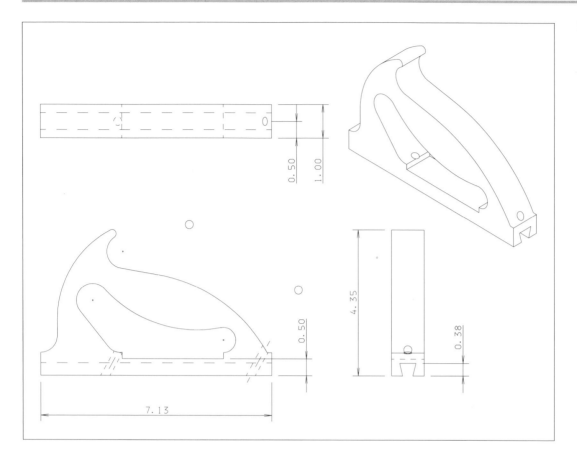

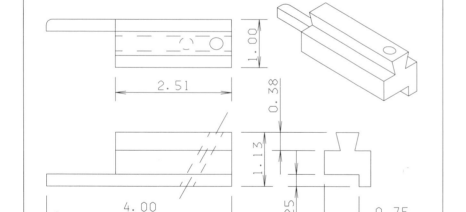

I usually use the long shoe and the thin shoe with a featherboard. The thin shoe, shown on page 71, is notched to push the workpiece through the cutter. It ends up being very similar to the saw's push handle.

Fence Holders

To keep the fences somewhat out of the way when they are not being used, attaching eyebolts to the station's side is a good solution. First install 1/4" threaded inserts in the side, then screw the eyebolts into the inserts. The fence's clamping slots position over the eyebolt's shaft, and the top eye bolt is turned to hold the fence against the side. Since the bottom eyebolt is only a peg to support the fence, you can use a dowel for this peg. The advantage of using an eyebolt for the bottom peg is that the round surface doesn't hurt as much when your leg bumps into it. An eyebolt is also stronger than a dowel. This method of attachment is shown in a number of the earlier photographs.

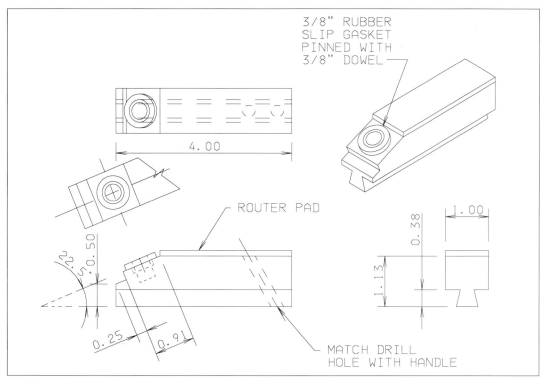

3/8" RUBBER SLIP GASKET PINNED WITH 3/8" DOWEL

ROUTER PAD

MATCH DRILL HOLE WITH HANDLE

PUSH BLOCK—SHORT SHOE

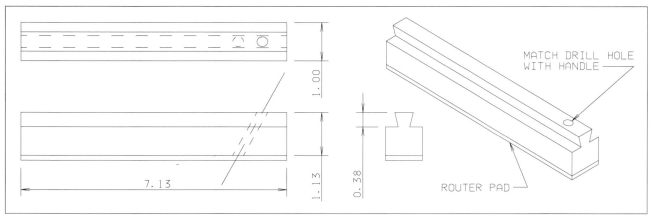

MATCH DRILL HOLE WITH HANDLE

ROUTER PAD

PUSH BLOCK—LONG SHOE

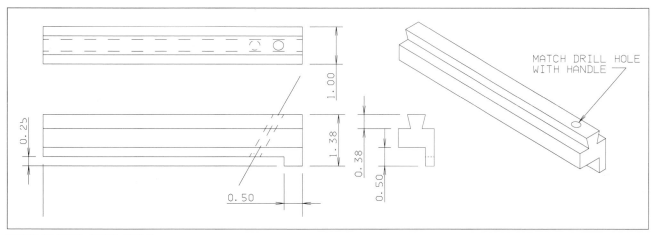

MATCH DRILL HOLE WITH HANDLE

PUSH BLOCK—THIN SHOE

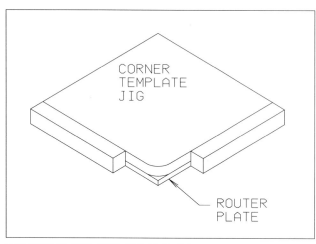

ROUTER PLATE AND CORNER JIG

Corner Jig

This is not a matter of taking a shortcut while square dancing but of rounding off square corners. When making your own router plates, you can either square the corners of the plate recess, which was cut with the ⅜" rabbet bit in the router station top, or you can round the corners of the plate. This rounding can be simplified if you make the simple jig shown above.

Using ½" birch plywood, cut a square with roughly a 7" side. Now carefully cut a ⅜" radius at one corner so that it mates with the corners of the router plate opening. If your first radius isn't just right, try again on another corner. When you have it right, glue two ¾" x ¾" x 5" strips onto the sides. Make sure there is no glue buildup on the inside corners. The router plate you are making must sit flat and square in the jig.

After the glue has set, clamp the jig to one corner of the square plate. This is your router pattern.

Using a top-bearing pattern router bit, rout away the protruding corner. Repeat for the other three corners. If the square piece you just trimmed is the cover plate for the router plate opening, and if the fit is good, your cover plate is now a good template for trimming new router plates. This is a template that can be used anytime, and the beauty of it is that it's not just another jig that you don't know what to do with when it's not needed.

The corner jig that you used could be thrown away, but don't do it. This type of jig is handy to have around. You may even want to make more of them with varying radii.

Chapter six describes an even more advanced router fence system.

Drawings, Cutting List and Materials List

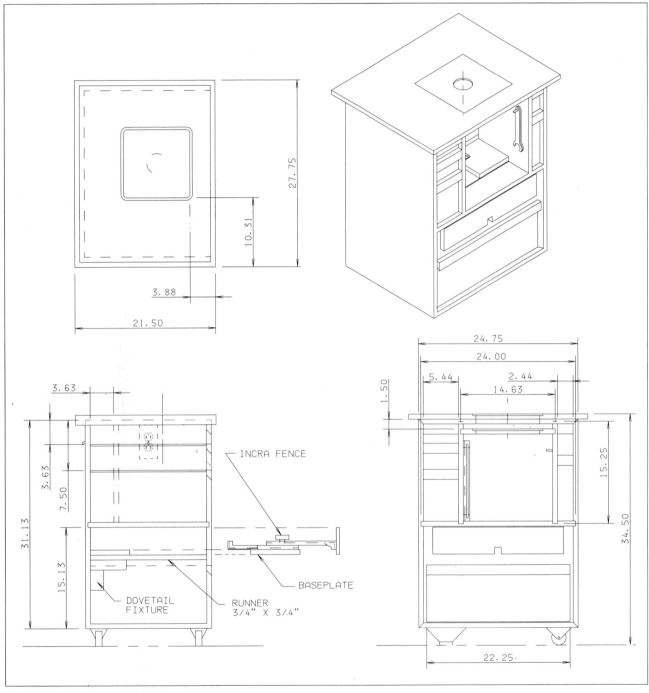

OUTLINE AND DIMENSIONED DRAWINGS

HARDWARE

PART	QTY	DESCRIPTION	SOURCE	COMMENTS
Wheels	2	Casters, 2" swivel	Woodworker's Supply PN. 812-958	
Wheels	2	Casters, 2" fixed	Woodworker's Supply PN. 812-965	
Slide	1 pr.	20" slides	Woodworker's Supply PN. 878-239	
Inserts	4	¼" x 20 threaded	Woodworker's Supply	
Toggle Clamp	1	Vertical Clamp	Woodworker's Supply PN. 812-304	Special Miter
Toggle Clamp	1	Horizontal Clamp	Woodworker's Supply PN. 173-005	Vertical Miter
Romex		14 gauge with ground		
Double Gang Receptacle Box	4			
15-amp Double Receptacle	1			
2 Outlet Cover Plate	1			
Switch Plate	2			
Male Base	1	Flanged inlet and outlet (Alt.—Nylon cup male base PN. 5278)	Sylvania Wiring Devices PN. P29911	Alt. Bryant, Milford, CT (800) 323-2792
Switch— 3-Position	2			
Clock Receptacle	1	775 V-Box NEMA 5-15R	Eagle Electric	Use for router power connection

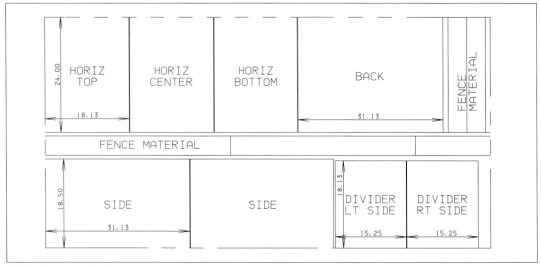

CUTTING DIAGRAM

Cutting List

CARCASE—See Cutting Diagram

PART	QTY	DESCRIPTION	MATERIAL	COMMENTS
Back	1	31.13" x 24.00" (31⅛" x 24")	¾" Shop Birch	
Side	2	31.13" x 18.50" (31⅛" x 18½")	¾" Shop Birch	Right and Left
Horizontals	3.	24.00" x 18.13" (24" x 18⅛")	¾" Shop Birch	Dadoes and cutouts define particular position.
Divider—Right and Left	2	15.25" x 18.13" (15¼" x 18⅛")	¾" Shop Birch	
Divider—Ctr	1	15.25" x 14.63" (15¼" x 14⅝")	¾" Shop Birch	
Runners	2	¾" x ¾" x required length (cut to fit)	Hardwood	Tray Supports
Trim	—	¾" x ¾" border trim. Approximately 3' x 8"—Same material will be used for drawer pulls and other trims.	Hardwood	Pick wood color desired—contrasting or blending.
Router Holder	—	Use scrap cuts	¾" Shop Birch	
Plate Holder	—	Use scrap cuts	¾" Shop Birch	

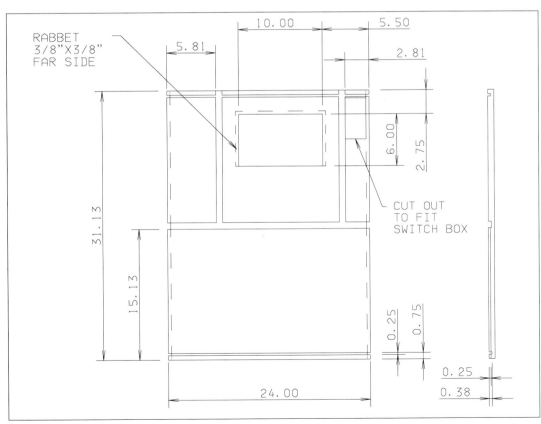

BACK

DRAWERS

PART	QTY	DESCRIPTION	MATERIAL	COMMENTS
Top Drawer	1			
Front/Back	2	5.44" x 2.88" (5⁷⁄₁₆" x 2⅞")	½" Baltic birch plywood	
Side	2.	2.88" x 17.75" (2⅞" x 17¾")	¼" 5 layer plywood	
Bottom	1	5.19" x 17.50" (5³⁄₁₆" x 17½")	⅛" hardboard	
Center Drawer	1			
Front/Back	2	5.44" x 3.63" (5⁷⁄₁₆" x 3⅝")	½" Baltic birch plywood	
Side	2	3.63" x 17.75" (3⅝" x 17¾")	¼" 5 layer plywood	
Bottom	1	5.19" x 17.50" (5³⁄₁₆" x 17½")	⅛" hardboard	
Lower Drawer	1			
Front/Back	2	5.44" x 7.50" (5⁷⁄₁₆" x 7½")	½" Baltic birch plywood	
Side	2	7.50" x 17.75" (7½" x 17¾")	¼" 5 layer plywood	
Bottom	1	5.19" x 17.50" (5³⁄₁₆" x 17½")	⅛" hardboard	
Bottom Drawer	1			
Front	1	8.63" x 23.00" (8⅝" x 23")	½" Baltic birch plywood	
Back	1	5.00" x 22.25" (5" x 22¼")	½" Baltic birch plywood	
Side	2	8.63" x 17.75" (8⅝" x 17¾")	½" Baltic birch plywood	
Bottom	1	21.75" x 17.00" (21¾" x 17")	½" Baltic birch plywood	
Bit Drawer	1			
Front/Back	1	2.50" x 8.75" (2½" x 8¾")	½" Baltic birch plywood	
Side	4	2.50" x 17.75" (2½" x 17¾")	½" Baltic birch plywood	
Back	2	8" x 17"	⅛" or ¼" hardboard	
Bit Bar	2	1.50" x 16.25" (1½" x 16¼")	1" (¾") hardwood	
Drawer Pulls	5	1.5" x 45.00" (1½" x 45")	1" (¾") hardwood	Pick wood color desired—contrasting or blending.

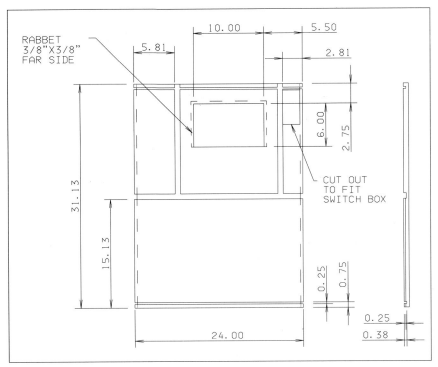

RABBET
3/8"X3/8"
FAR SIDE

CUT OUT
TO FIT
SWITCH BOX

SIDES

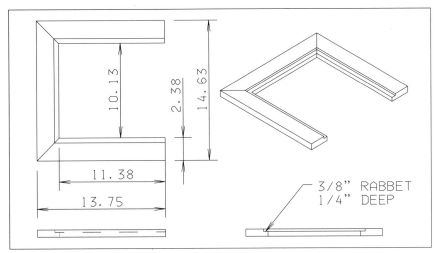

3/8" RABBET
1/4" DEEP

ROUTER HOLDER

TOP

PART	QTY	DESCRIPTION	MATERIAL	COMMENTS
Base	1	26.25" x 20.00" (26¼" x 20")	¾" Shop Birch	See section in chapter one on "Workstation Tops."
Borders	—	1.50" x 100.00" (1½" x 100")	¾" hardwood	Pick wood color desired—contrasting or blending.
Top Surface	1	26.75" x 20.50" (26¾" x 20½")		See section in chapter one on "Workstation Tops."

HORIZONTALS

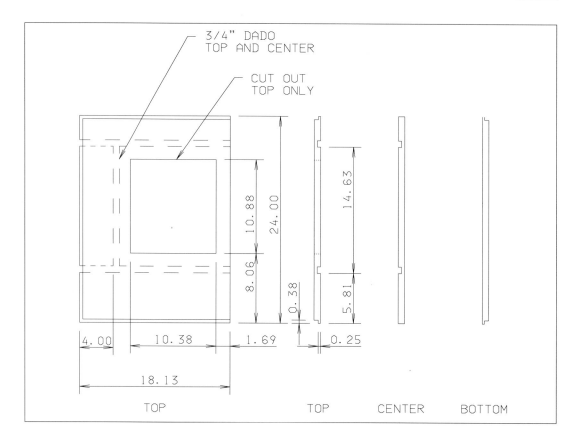

DIVIDERS

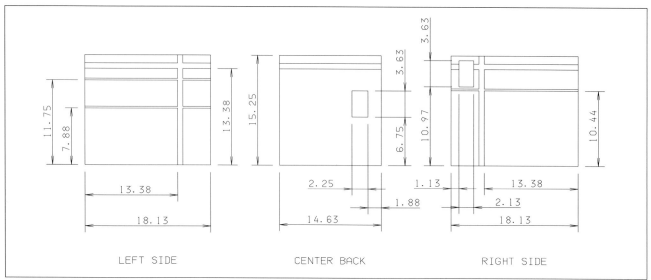

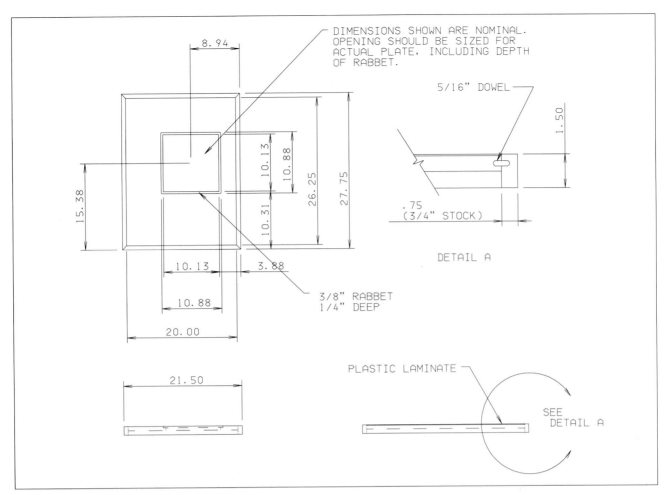

DIMENSIONS SHOWN ARE NOMINAL.
OPENING SHOULD BE SIZED FOR
ACTUAL PLATE, INCLUDING DEPTH
OF RABBET.

5/16" DOWEL

8.94

15.38

10.13
10.88
26.25
27.75
10.31
10.88

10.13   3.88

10.88

20.00

3/8" RABBET
1/4" DEEP

1.50

.75
(3/4" STOCK)

DETAIL A

21.50

PLASTIC LAMINATE

SEE
DETAIL A

TOP

UPPER DRAWERS

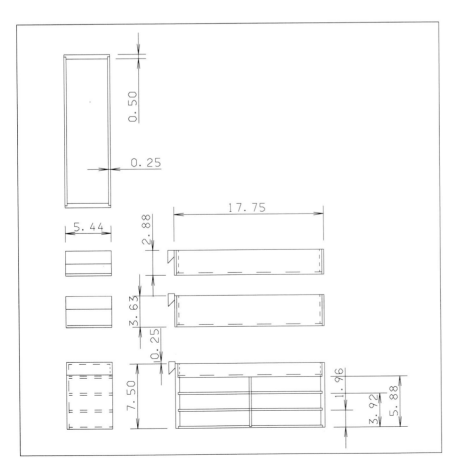

0.50

0.25

5.44

2.88

17.75

3.63

0.25

7.50

1.96

5.88

3.92

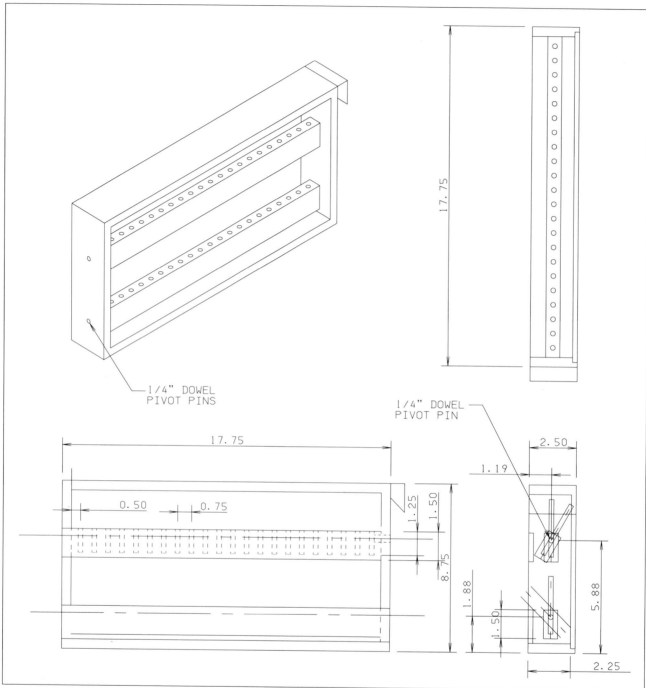

1/4" DOWEL PIVOT PINS

1/4" DOWEL PIVOT PIN

17.75

17.75

0.50   0.75

1.25   1.50

8.75

1.88

1.50

2.50

1.19

5.88

2.25

BIT DRAWER

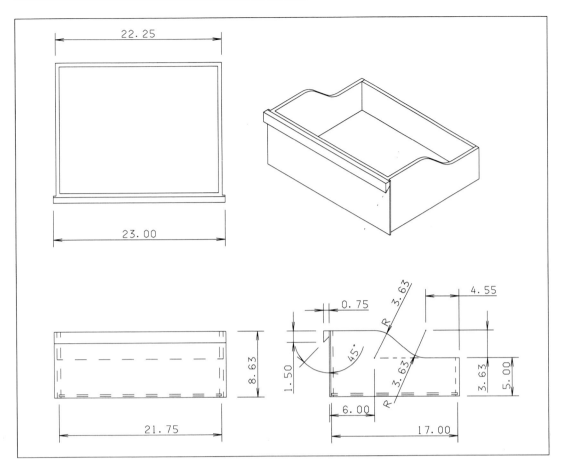

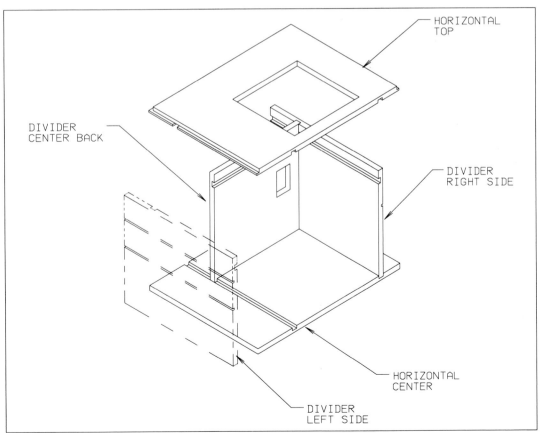

SUBASSEMBLY ASSEMBLY

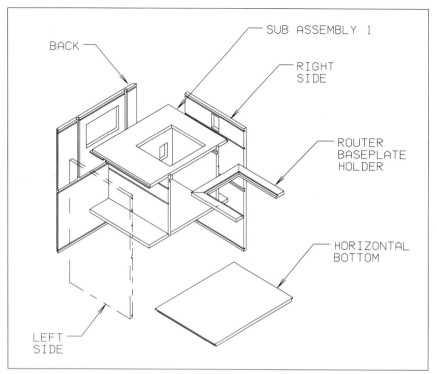

CARCASE ASSEMBLY

THE ASSEMBLY WORKSTATION

ASSEMBLY WORKSTATION

The assembly workstation, like the table saw workstation, is designed as a support station that holds the tools used in assembly. For me these tools have included screwdrivers, drills, drill motors, a saber saw, and an ample collection of fasteners and related hardware. Since building the first assembly workstation, I have built a number of variations, including stations for drafting, layout, and my good woodworking tools; a station for power tools (this is the first station I reorganized); and with a rather major modification, a station for finishing. I even have a half-sized version (one drawer wide) that holds nothing but hardware. This half-sized variation is shown and discussed after I describe the basic design.

Organization

The basic assembly station is a chest of drawers. And like the table saw station, it has a hinged cover that can be used for the storage of frequently used tools.

For the first station, the tools I chose to be close at hand were screwdrivers (a slotted head and a Phillips), a cordless drill/driver, a try square, calipers, a backsaw and a scratch awl. I added other tools and holders over time.

These were the 20 percent tools used 80 percent of the time in my assembly work. The other tools, and particularly the larger tools, were stored in the drawers or in the upper compartment. Again, as in the table saw workstation, a pullout tray was incorporated into the upper compartment to facilitate quick movement of the collected paraphernalia when the top had to be closed.

In laying out the top, a No. 7 slotted head and No. 2 Phillips screwdrivers were chosen for quick access. All the other screwdrivers were stored in the drawers.

The cordless drill/driver is the Craftsman model 315.111240. It is an exclusive Craftsman design and one that I think is excellent. Features that are particularly appealing are the forward/reverse trigger switch and the bit storage in the handle. As purchased, it has only one bad feature: the wrist strap. This strap can easily catch on other tools or workpieces when it is being picked up. This strap should be removed to avoid accidents.

The try square is the 8" Stanley model 20TS, and the caliper is another General Tools black on yellow. This Stanley try square has an engraved scale on the blade that makes it handy for laying out screw holes. I selected a reversible offset backsaw as the most versatile for small end cutting and cutting dowels. I use the scratch awl primarily for punching starter holes.

Many computers are organized with what is called "cache memory." Cache memory is simply an organization of what's stored close at hand and quickly available. If the processor is using a particular file, the cache logic assumes that the processor will want the related (close by) files. Since "fast" memory is expensive and "slow memory" is cheap, cache logic will try to keep what is being used most of the time in fast memory and leave the rest in slow memory.

Your assembly workstation has a cache memory. Hardware is stored in trays (files). The trays and the hardware you use most are stored in the small (fast)

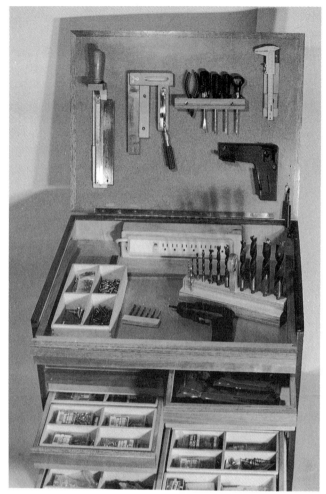

TRAYS FOR HARDWARE STORAGE
As shown here the drawers are used both for hardware and for tool storage. The removable trays can be moved to the top tray or to other work areas. The hinged top holds frequently used tools that are small enough to fit in the space. The other tools used in assembly are kept in the drawers.

upper drawers. The other trays and their hardware contents are stored below in the larger and less accessible (slow) drawers. The system works, especially if you don't clutter up your memory with obsolete or infrequently used files (hardware). When you are using No. 8 flathead screws, pull up the tray that has the various lengths of No. 8 flatheads.

The trays can be built with dividers, depending on what is being stored.

Knowing that you have such a state-of-the-art design incorporated into your station, you may find the rest of the assembly workstation's features to be somewhat prosaic. After all, how much can be said about more drawers? There are, however, some not-so-prosaic variations.

TRAY STYLES

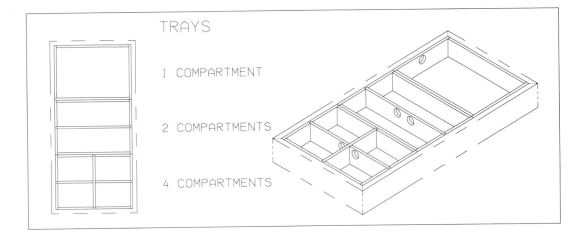

TRAYS

1 COMPARTMENT

2 COMPARTMENTS

4 COMPARTMENTS

Building the Assembly Workstation

The assembly workstation is similar to the table saw workstation and is constructed in an identical manner. The principal difference between them is in the division of the space and the number of drawers.

If you want to use biscuits instead of the dado/glue construction, remember to adjust the cutting dimensions. With either method of construction, you can save on both wood and weight by using frame construction for the interior horizontals.

The Carcase Dado/Glue Construction

The order or sequence of assembling the parts is this:

1. Position back.
2. Place center horizontal.
3. Add top horizontal.

4. Put in drawer dividers.
5/6. Position sides.
7. Slide in bottom horizontal.

This sequence is illustrated on page 86.

With all of the workstations, it's a good idea to clean the rabbets and dadoes before gluing.

This completes the carcase assembly. As before, mount the wheels, then cut and glue on the trim strips.

After the glue has set, flush the edges using the methods previously described. If you haven't done it yet, you should cut the electrical opening now.

Chapter four, "The Sanding and Gluing Station," describes how to use that station for plate jointing. You may want to review the techniques described there before you start to construct the assembly station. You may also want to consider using a hybrid construction of both plate and dado/glue joints.

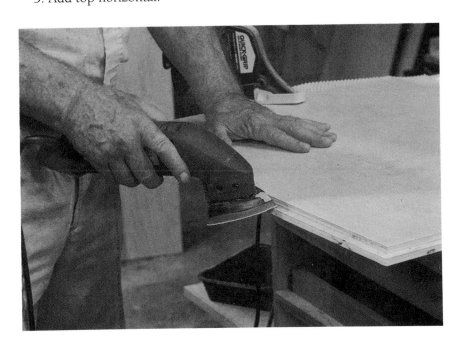

SANDING THE EDGES
Cleaning the rabbets with a detail sander before assembly is worthwhile. After the glue has been applied, tight joints can become very tight—in some cases, too tight.

Power Strip Box

The power strip box serves two functions: (1) It lets you mount the power strip at an angle that facilitates the plugging and unplugging of the power tools, and (2) it becomes a box for storing the strip's power cord.

The box is quickly made using ½" stock (plywood or solid) for the end caps and ¼" plywood for the covers. The end caps are rabbeted to position the cover strips and allow a flush mounting to the caps. A slot is cut in one end cap to accept the power strip's power cord.

Attachment of the power strip box is best accomplished with screws through the back. Using screws makes the box removable.

Access Cover Door

The access cover door is cut from ¾" plywood sized to fit the previously cut opening and attached to the case with a length of piano hinge. The power cord is folded and tucked behind the door when not in use.

Making the Holders

Three new holders are needed for the assembly station. The others are repeats. In the case of the cordless drill/driver, the holder comes with the drill.

Back Saw Bracket

I designed the bracket on page 89 to hold the back saw. This bracket will hold the saw in either of its two cutting positions and can be mounted vertically or

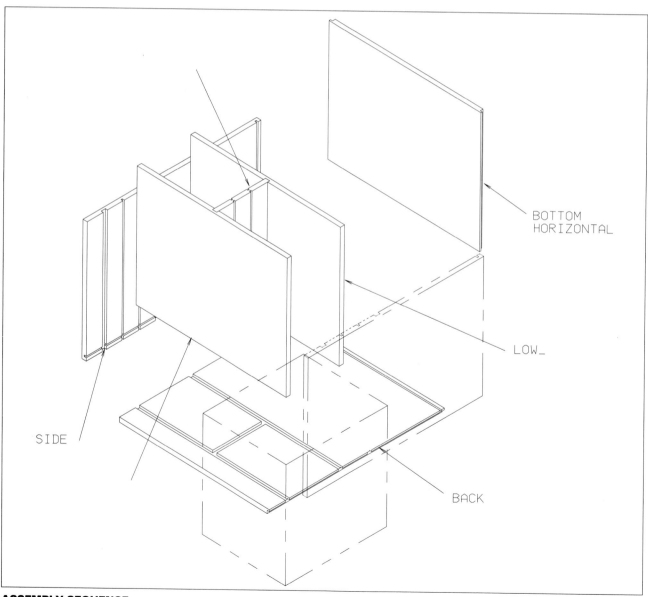

BOTTOM
HORIZONTAL

LOW_

SIDE

BACK

ASSEMBLY SEQUENCE

horizontally. A magnet on a stand-off plate holds the saw blade.

Screwdriver Rack

The other new holder is a simple strip for the screwdrivers, scratch awl, and the other tools you want handy. This bracket can be made to any size that will fit on the top. The size will depend on what you want to have available. The holes for the screwdrivers and similar items often hold them more securely if they are sized to fit both the blade and the ferrule of the tool, as shown below.

Drill Bit Block

A drill block for holding an 11-piece set of brad point drills can be made to fit an assembly station drawer. The drills lie flat when stored and the drawer is closed.

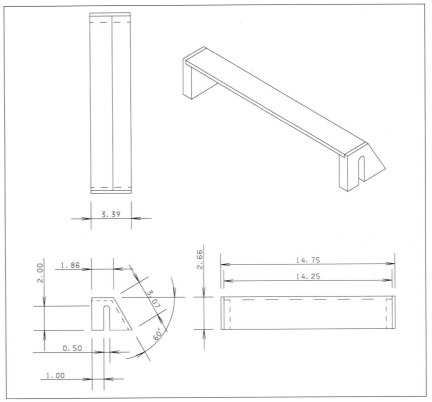

POWER STRIP BOX

When the drawer is opened, the drill block can be set to an upright position for easy access. If you use any drawers other than the top ones, the drill bits in the upright position will not protrude above the station's top surface.

The block is laid out for seven bits with collars, ⅛" through ½", and for the four larger bits, ⅝", ¾", ⅞" and 1", without collars. The forward portion of the block can be used to hold the ½²" and ¹⁄₁₆" drills or any other odd sizes you have and need a place for.

The holes drilled in the block to hold the drill bits are the drill chuck shaft diameter plus ¹⁄₆₄". This allows the drill to be removed easily without binding. To keep the drill bits from being too loose in the block, drill the final ¼" depth of the hole with the actual chuck shaft diameter. For the ⅜" through 1" drills, this final hole is drilled with a ⅜" bit. This gives the right amount of grab without undue binding.

The block can be hinge-pinned to the drawer, but if you do, you can't pick up the set of drills and carry them to another station or tool.

Trays

Hardware and other small parts are stored in trays. The basic tray is shown on page 92.

Since lots of trays are being recommended, some

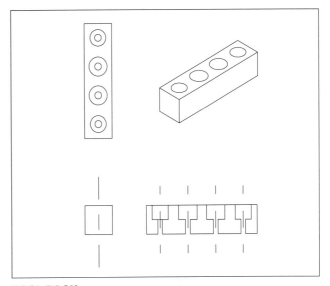

TOOL RACK

production-type jig to make these drawers is in order.

There are two primary reasons for building a jig. One is to ensure an accurate, safe cut. The other is to speed up repetitive work. The box joint for the trays benefits from the latter. The construction of the assembly workstation calls for at least 12 trays. For the box joint specified, there will be 4 cuts per box end, 2 ends per side, 4 sides per box, and 12 boxes for the station. That's a total of 384 cuts to make these

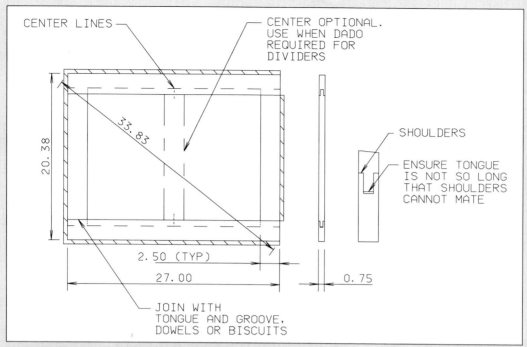

HORIZONTALS— SAVING WOOD

SAVING WOOD AND WEIGHT

It's possible to save a lot of wood and weight by making some of the horizontals using frame construction. This is a good use for the leftover shop birch that you don't want to throw away but have no real use for. The tongue-and-groove joint is the easiest to make and can be made on the saw or with your router. If you use the router, it's best to have a set of tongue-and-groove cutters.

Building the frame also illustrates a number of "good shop practices" that should be applied to all of your cutting and construction.

With tongue-and-groove joints, always mark one surface of each piece and keep this face up or against the saw fence when you are making the cuts. If the cutter or saw path is not at the exact center, the joined surfaces will still be flush. Also, make sure that the tongue is not so long that it keeps the shoulders of the tongue from resting firmly against the shoulder of the grooved piece. Observe this rule for the carcase joints used in building the workstations. The same thing is, of course, true for dowel joints; if the dowel is too long, you can't properly mate the pieces. This is the exception to accepted mating practices.

When the plans call for a dado in the horizontal's center, include a center span. Position the center span by marking its center and aligning the center mark with the centers of the rails. This results in a more accurate placement of the spanner than you would get when using edge distances for its placement.

To ensure a square and dimensionally accurate horizontal frame, it's a good idea to cut the pieces slightly oversized. When the glue has set, you can trim the complete piece on the saw. To aid in this trimming, one stile should have a slight offset with respect to the rail so that, when you cut, a continuous surface rides the fence. If the rail protrudes and interferes with the stile, clamp a framing square to the piece and let the framing square leg ride the fence. This setup is shown here.

To make sure that you don't end up with a parallelogram, check the diagonals of the finished piece. For the example here, both diagonals should be 33.82". The length of the diagonal is calculated using the Pythagorean theorem where $R2 = X2 + Y2$ (Diagonal2 = 272" + 20.382"). This same technique should be used to check the squareness of drawers, carcases, or any right angle form.

CUTTING THE TONGUE AND GROOVES

The quickest way to cut the tongue-and-groove joints is to use tongue-and-groove cutters at the router station. You can also use the table saw, but that will take more time.

SAVING

If you need to trim a parallelogram into a rectangle and the workpiece is too large for the saw's miter, you can use a framing square. Make sure the framing square's arm clears the saw blade.

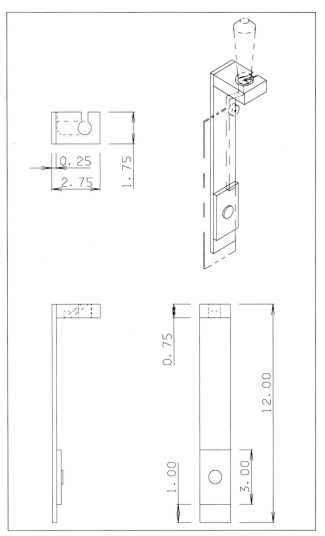

BACK SAW BRACKET

joints. If we assume that each cut will take 15 seconds, then it will take 3.2 hours to make all of the cuts. On the other hand, if a jig can be made that requires, say, 45 seconds per cut but only needs 16 cuts, then all of the cuts can be made in 45 seconds x 16 cuts = 720 seconds, or 12 minutes (.2 hours). If we can make the jig in less than three hours, we are saving time and making something that can be used in future projects.

Variations in Design

The variations in layout of the assembly workstation are infinite. It can be designed for more or fewer drawers, larger or smaller drawers, or drawers designed for special tools or applications. One example is shown here. This workstation caddy is a half-sized assembly station with nothing but drawers. Another variation, the custom workstation, is described in chapter six.

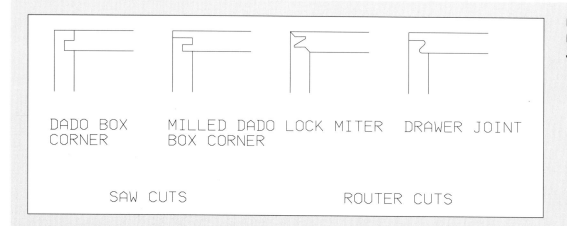

EXAMPLES OF DRAWER JOINTS

DADO BOX CORNER   MILLED DADO BOX CORNER   LOCK MITER   DRAWER JOINT

SAW CUTS   ROUTER CUTS

MAKING THE DRAWERS

Most of the drawers are constructed from ½" Baltic birch plywood or ½" almaciga. Any of the seven or more layer plywoods can be used. What is nice about the almaciga is that, after oiling and coating, it has such a rich look. In most cases, these multilayered plywoods can be machined or cut like solid wood. The birch, which I am familiar with (it's customarily marked Finnish birch), has a thick enough veneer to allow a reasonable amount of sanding.

The drawer joint used for the sides can be a dado box corner like the case, or a milled box corner, or it can be cut with the router using either a lock miter or a drawer joint router bit. The drawer joint router bit allows you to cut a rabbeted offset face. This makes it more versatile than the lock miter. Getting a lock miter bit for ½" stock can also pose a problem, whereas the drawer joint or (as Sears calls it) the box joint bit is readily available. I don't recommend using a dovetail joint with the plywood because it doesn't machine that well. I also don't recommend using a dovetail unless you are going for appearance. Dovetails take longer to cut, and the strength of the joint isn't warranted by itself for this application. The recommended joints are shown here.

The drawers that are on slides should have a rabbeted offset front to hide the slides. To create this rabbeted offset, you can use ¾" stock for the drawer's front face or reinforce the resulting lip by gluing on a backup strip after the drawer has been assembled and glued. The lip that results from the drawer joint bit when you use ½" stock will be less than ⅛" thick. It can be easily broken unless the backup strip is added. For the small drawers, any of the joints shown will work fine. To me, a drawer is a tray (bottom) with sides around it to keep things from falling out. This viewpoint is reflected in the designs.

Before man-made boards were available, drawer construction had to account for wood movement and the tools being used. We no longer have these constraints and should take advantage of the freedom offered with the new materials. Make the bottoms with true square corners and then use them to position the sides and glue the bottom to the sides. You should still check the squareness of the glued-up assembly since the drawers must be exactly sized to fit the openings in the station carcase. The small drawers don't need runners or slides. As long as the station is square, and you haven't left any glue buildup along the inside edges in the carcase, the

HEIGHT OF OPENING (2.75")

WIDTH OF OPENING (12.75")

2.75

0.19

BOTTOM DIMENSIONS

SMALL DRAWER

drawers will slide just fine.

Proof of a good fit is when you have to drill air escape holes in the backs of the drawers. The drawer acts like a piston, and if you have a really good fit, the trapped air will start to compress before it can escape. This makes opening and closing the drawer something of a chore.

BUILDING THE DRAWERS—SMALL DRAWERS

The height and width dimensions for the small drawers are taken from the height and width of the openings that will accept these drawers. In some cases, variation of the plywood sheet from the nominal ¾" used in making the station must be compensated in determining the drawer size dimensions. By measuring the openings and using the measured dimensions to construct the drawers, this variation is corrected. The length and width of the drawer sides will depend on the type of corner joint selected. See illustration on page 90.

The drawer sides are made from ½" plywood and the bottoms from ¼" hardboard or KorTron. The exception is the drawers used in the router station. For these drawers, ¼" birch plywood is used for the sides and ½" plywood for the ends. This was done primarily to increase the drawers' inside dimensions.

The white KorTron makes a drawer bottom that is attractive in appearance and easy to clean. I use this material for the bottoms of kitchen drawers and always have some around. For the sides of these kitchen drawers, I use either ½" solid hardwood with dovetail corners (a rabbeted dovetail for the front) or almaciga plywood with lock miter corners. When I use the almaciga, I screw a separate drawer face to the drawer box.

For the small drawers in the workstations, I prefer the lock miter joint. If you follow this suggestion, you may want to wait to make the drawers until you have built the router station. The drawer pulls are easier to cut out with the saw.

DRAWER PULLS

The drawer pulls are simple and effective. They are cut from ¾" x 1½" hardwood stock. The best way to make the pulls is to form a long piece of stock and then cut off the required lengths.

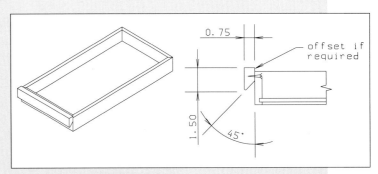

EXAMPLE OF DRAWER PULLS

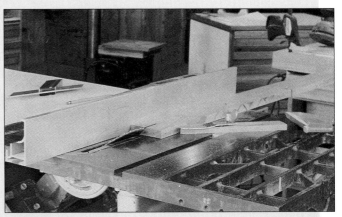

CUTTING THE PULLS
The best way to cut the drawer pulls is to cut the pairs from wider stock. Don't try to be exact with the cut's width. Just make it a little oversized and then trim to required width.

ATTACHING THE PULLS
Set the pulls to the required height, either flush or up ¼", and fasten with screws.

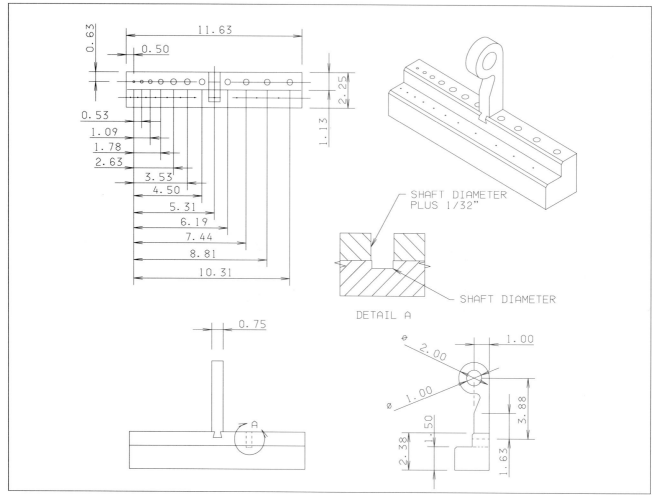

DRILL BIT BLOCK

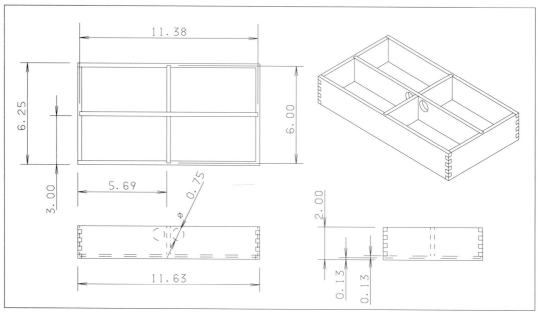

BASIC TRAY DESIGN

WORKSTATION CADDY

This workstation caddy is a half-sized assembly station that can support any shop need. The three top drawers are interchangeable with the top drawers of the assembly-style stations and with the table saw station. Most shoe boxes will fit in the lower drawers and can be used as trays and separators for all the "other stuff" that tends to collect in every shop.

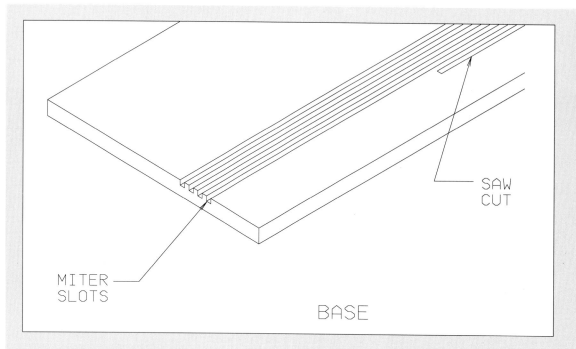

BASE FOR SPECIAL MITER FENCE

SAW CUT

MITER SLOTS

BASE

BOX JOINT CUTTING JIG

The jig has two parts: a base and a special miter fence. The base is actually a top that replaces the saw top. It has multiple miter slots to accept and guide the special miter fence. This special miter holds and positions the tray sides as the waste between the pins is cut, while the miter fence rides in the slots cut in the base. These two parts are shown here.

The base is made from ¾" MDF. When you cut the miter slots, which are ¼" dadoes, make sure that the spacing is exact. To do this, use the ¼" strips as spacers to position the base against the fence; these strips will later be cut into tray sides.

Start with eight side strips between the fence and the base. The first cut will be the blade path followed when you make the box joint cuts. Raise the dado blades for a through cut and cut into the base about 12". Now lower the blade for a ⁵⁄₃₂"-deep dado cut, remove two spacers, or sides, flip the base on its longitudinal axis, and reposition it against the fence. The base is flipped because the dadoes are cut with the base face down, whereas the first cut was made with the face up. Holding the base firmly against the spacers, make the first miter slot cut.

Continue removing pairs of spacers, repositioning the base against the fence and making miter slots until all of the slots have been cut. This completes the base construction.

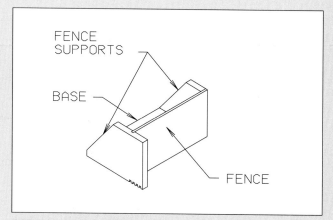

FENCE SUPPORTS

BASE

FENCE

SPECIAL MITER FENCE

The special miter fence is similar to a tenon jig but does not ride on the fence or in one of the saw's miter slots; instead, it rides in the miter slots that were cut in the base. The jig's fence supports and base are made from ¾" plywood. The fence is made from the same ¼" stock that is used for the tray sides. Cut two fences. One will be permanently attached to the special miter fence, and the other will be used as a spacer when cutting one set of tray sides. The fence is attached to the supports and base and protrudes ¼" below the jig's base, becoming the jig's miter bar.

Before you cut the sides, it's a good idea to check the height of the dado blade and the width of its cut. Shim the blades for a snug but not too-tight fit and

set the height ⅟₃₂" over the thickness of the sides. Nominally this
will be ¼" + ⅟₃₂" = ⁹⁄₃₂". The protruding pins will be sanded flush
after the tray has been assembled
and glued. If the sides are cut to
the measured dimension the resultant width and length will be ⅟₁₆"
less than the opening, a good tolerance to have.

Measure the inside dimension
of the drawers that will be holding
the trays. They should all be the
same, but if they're not, use the
smallest dimension so that any
tray can fit in any drawer. Cut the
tray sides and ends from strips
that have been ripped to the
required height. Use a stop block
on your miter for this operation so
that all the sides are the same
length and all the ends are the
same length.

Stack all of the long tray sides
together into a block and, using
masking tape, tape them together,
then clamp this taped block to the
fence. Position the base on the saw
using the through cut or blade
path to position it with respect to
the dado blades. Bring the saw's
fence against its right side for support and alignment and then
clamp the base to the saw table.
Place the fence tongue (miter bar)
in the first slot and make the first
cut. Continue until all of the pins
have been cut, then flip the block
of sides and cut the pins in the
other end.

For the other sides of the trays,
use the extra fence that was cut
earlier to offset this block's set of
pins.

If the pins have been cut too short, making the
tray too wide or too long, cut a recess in the other
side to compensate for the short pins.

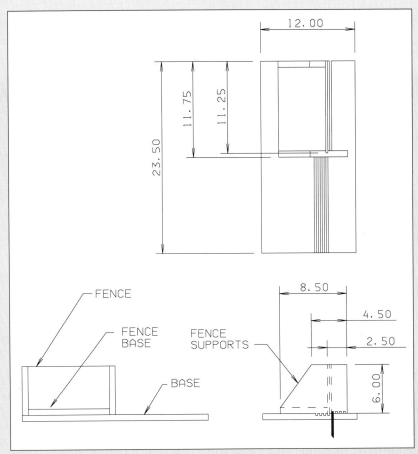

BASE AND SPECIAL MITER FENCE—DIMENSIONED DRAWING

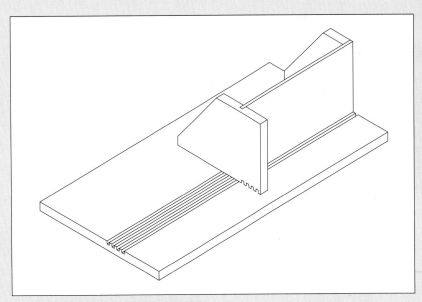

BASE AND SPECIAL MITRE FENCE

If the pins were cut too long, the tray bottom can
be used to establish the correct size. There will be a
slight gap between the ends and the side, but the
tray will still be strong enough and functional.

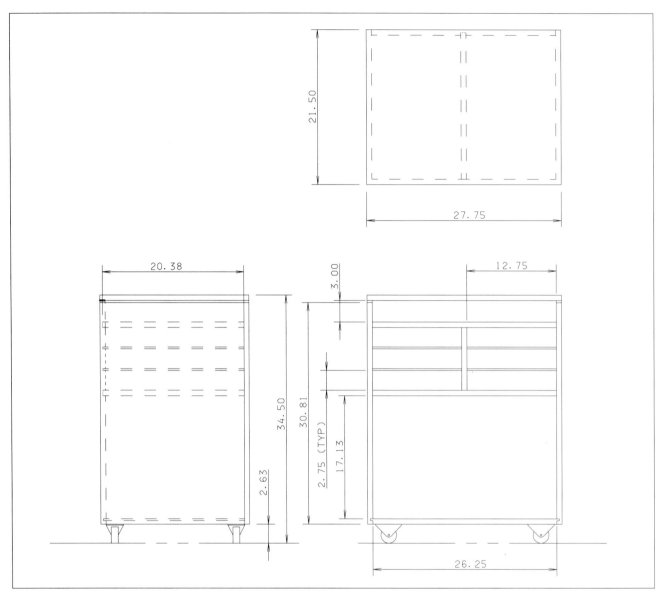

OUTLINE AND DIMENSION DRAWING

Drawings, Cutting List and Materials List

HARDWARE

PART	QTY	DESCRIPTION	SOURCE	COMMENTS
Wheels	4	Casters, 2 " swivel		
Lid Support	1	Use the high torque (95–125 inch/lbs.) style.	Woodworker's Supply PN. 100-041	Right or Left. Right PN. 100-040
Hinge	1	Piano Hinge — 1 1/16"		
Power Strip	1	7–15 amp, 125 V grounded outlets.		
Drawer Slide	2	20" Slide	Woodworker's Supply PN. 878-239	

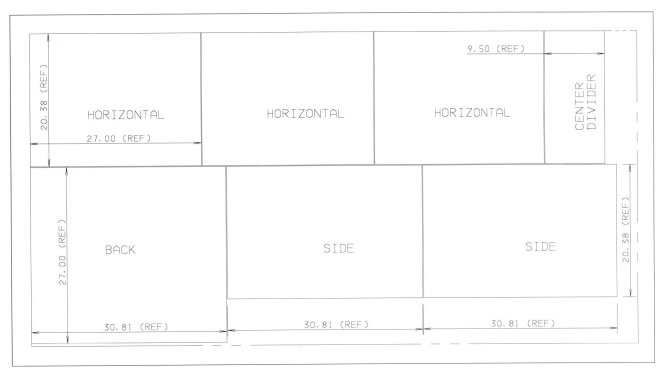

CUTTING DIAGRAM—DADO/GLUE CONSTRUCTION

CUTTING LIST Carcase—Dado/Glue Construction—See Cutting Diagram

PART	QTY	DESCRIPTION	MATERIAL	COMMENTS
Back	1	30.81" x 27.00" (30¹³⁄₁₆" x 27")	¾" Shop Birch	
Side	2	30.81" x 20.75" (30¹³⁄₁₆" x 20¾")	¾" Shop Birch	Right and Left
Horizontals	3	20.38" x 27.00" (20⅜" x 27")	¾" Shop Birch	Dadoes and cutouts define particular position.
Divider	1	20.38" x 9.50" (20⅜" x 9½")	¾" Shop Birch	
Trim	—	¾" x ¾" border trim. Approximately 3' x 8"—Same material will be used for drawer pulls and other trims.	Hardwood	Pick wood color desired—contrasting or blending.

DRAWERS

PART	QTY	DESCRIPTION	MATERIAL	COMMENTS
Small Drawer	6			
Front/Back	4	2.75" x 12.75" (2¾" x 12¾")	½" Baltic birch plywood	
Side	4	2.75" x 20.00" (2¾" x 20")	½" Baltic birch plywood	
Bottom	2	12.25" x 19.50" (12¼" x 19½")	¼" MDF, Hardboard or KorTron, etc.	
Lower Drawers				
Upper				
Front	1	6" x 26"	½" Baltic birch plywood	
Back	2	6.00" x 25.25" (6" x 25¼")	½" Baltic birch plywood	
Side	2	6" x 20"	½" Baltic birch plywood	
Bottom	1	24.75" x 19.50" (24¾" x 19½")	½" Baltic birch plywood	
Lower				
Front	1	9" x 26"	½" Baltic birch plywood	
Back	2	9.00" x 25.25" (9" x 25¼")	½" Baltic birch plywood	
Side	2	9" x 20"	½" Baltic birch plywood	
Bottom	1	24.75" x 19.50" (24¾" x 19½")	½" Baltic birch plywood	
Tray				
Front	1	3.00" x 26.25" (3" x 26¼")	½" Baltic birch plywood	Back cut for lid support
Side	2	2" x 20"	½" Baltic birch plywood	One side cut for lid support
Bottom	1	25.50" x 19.25" (25½" x 19¼")	¼" 5 layer plywood	
Drawer Pulls	8	1.50" x 120.00" (1½" x 120")	1" (¾") hardwood	Pick wood color desired—contrasting or blending.

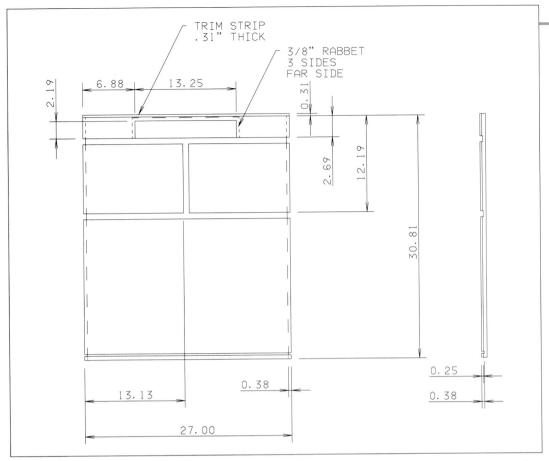

BACK

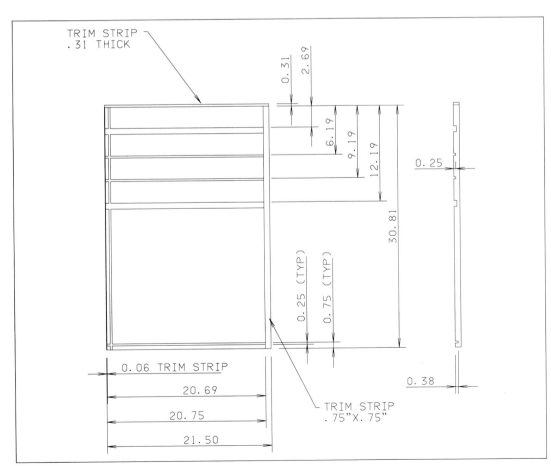

SIDES

TOP

PART	QTY	DESCRIPTION	MATERIAL	COMMENTS
Base	1	26.75" x 20.50" (26¾" x 20½")	¾" Shop Birch	See section on "Workstation Tops," page 16.
Borders	—	1.50" x 100.00" (1½" x 100")	¾" hardwood	Pick wood color desired—contrasting or blending.
Top Surface	1	26.75" x 20.50" (26¾" x 20½")		See section on "Workstation Tops," page 16.

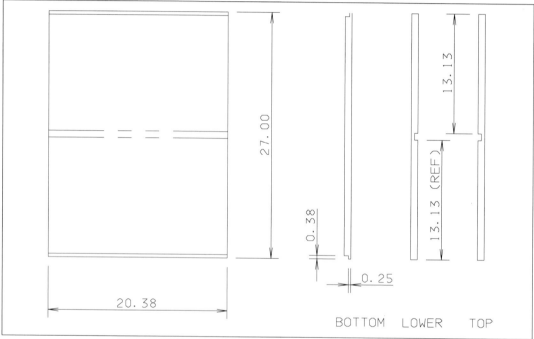

HORIZONTALS

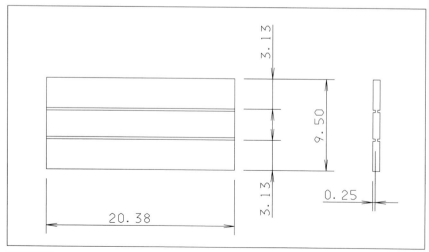

DIVIDER

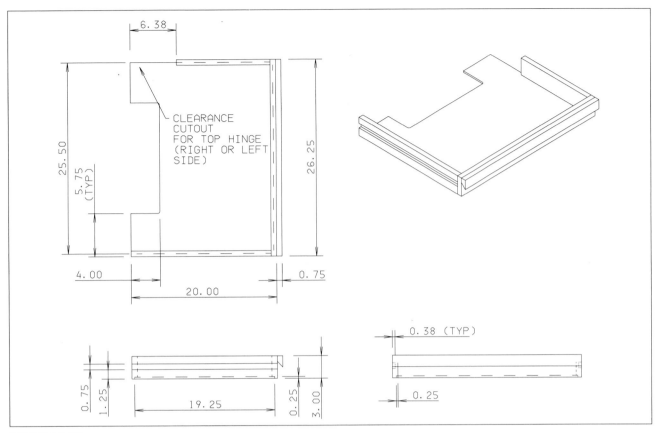

UPPER TRAY

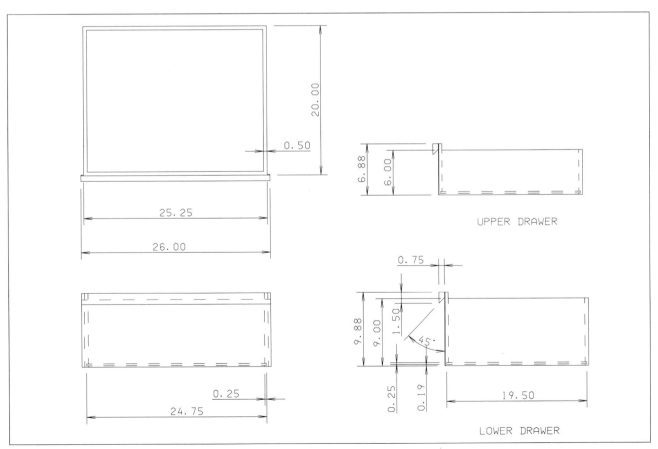

LARGE DRAWERS

CHAPTER FOUR

THE SANDING AND GLUING WORKSTATION

THE SANDING AND GLUING WORKSTATION

I like the sanding and gluing workstation. Its design has evolved from that of individual sanding and gluing benches I have used in the past. After I added some new features, the station became much more than a sanding and gluing bench; it is now a true work workstation. This station holds the workpiece so you can work on it and has shown itself to be particularly suitable for plate jointing.

The older features include the 2x4 standoffs, the adjustable clamping shelves and the extension table.

The new features are the Quick-Grip clamps, the combining of the clamping shelves with the station's drawers, and, of course, making it all fit together as a workstation. It works well.

Both the older gluing bench and sanding bench were low benches. To retain this height for certain work, an add-on work surface was incorporated in the form of a folding shelf on the side of the station.

The drawer design reflects its primary function as a clamping shelf. The bottom three drawers have separate clamping bars incorporated into their design; the two upper drawers use the clamping bar that is part of the top. These drawers, or clamping shelves, allow workpieces of widths up to 48" to be held and worked on. The drawers are actually more like boxes sitting on shelves.

The 2x4 standoffs are used to elevate the workpiece so that clamps can be used. These standoffs are similar to clamp blocks used with traditional woodworking benches. The clamp block dog pins are permanently attached and are inserted into holes in the station's top.

I have designed an extension table for use with the station. This folding table increases the work surface by over 4 square feet. If you plan to leave the station with its extension table set up, two other additions are warranted: a clothes-pole-type hanger for clamps and a drawer mounted to the extension table. It's easy to remove the pole, but you will have to find a place to put away the clamps. Unfortunately, when the runners for the drawer are added, they will keep the table's legs from folding flat.

My normal setup is to have the station with its extension table positioned behind the saw. Set like this it's a convenient work surface, and I can use the extension as the saw's infeed table.

Tools and supplies that I have stored in the sanding and gluing workstation include these:

6" Orbital Sander
4" Belt Sander
5" Finishing Sander
4⅜" Finishing Sander
Detail/Corner Sander (a rather new addition)
Sandpaper and Sanding Belts
Sander Accessories
Gluing Aids
Scrapers
Shavehooks
Sanding Blocks

Remember, a large part of my business is refinishing, and that means I need and use lots of sanding equipment. For the more typical home shop, one drawer dedicated to sanders probably will be enough. The other drawers can hold other tools. Think of this station as your primary workbench, which will have your primary woodworking tools, supported at the sides by the other stations.

Sandpaper and scrapers can be stored in the top compartment. This compartment, which has a hinged cover, is not particularly accessible and should only be used for storage. Don't store something here that you will want to get at after you have clamped your current project to the station's top—because you won't be able to.

The height of this compartment will accommodate a box of hook-and-loop disks but nothing much taller. There is lots of room for 9" x 11" sheets of sandpaper. Sanding belts can be stored in one of drawers.

Scrapers are valuable tools, and if they're not part of your tool collection, they should be. Woodcraft, a mail-order supplier of better tools and hardware,

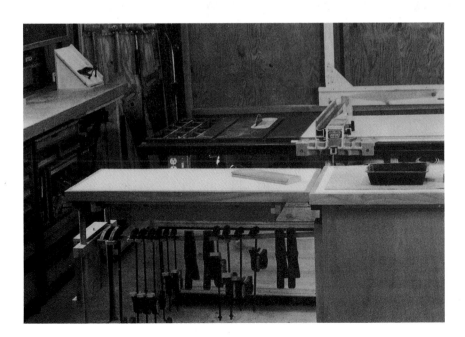

RELATIONSHIP BETWEEN THE POSITION OF SAW AND SANDING AND GLUING WORKSTATION

The sanding and gluing station with its extension table makes a convenient backup bench for the saw. As you can see, the extension table is positioned as an infeed table that is used for ripping 4x8 sheets. Under the extension table is a clothes-hanger-type pole for storing clamps. This particular view of the shop also shows one way to arrange the workstations and the Workmate for storage. The Workmate rolls straight out, becoming the saw's outfeed table.

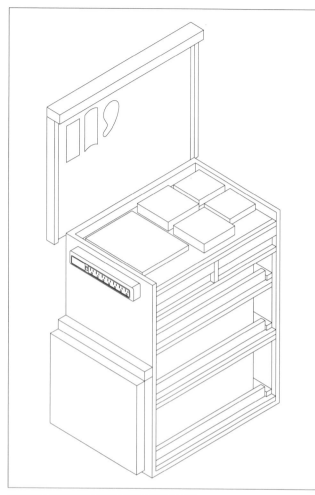

UPPER COMPARTMENT STORAGE

The station's primary purpose is clamping, which leaves the top area for use as storage. The space is not large and not easy to get at when the station is being used, but it is a good place to store sandpaper and the cabinet scrapers. To protect their edges, the scrapers are mounted on magnets.

offers a data sheet on cabinet scrapers, their uses, and how to sharpen them. This data sheet is identified as Publication 77A09, dated 10/26/90, and is included with any scraper ordered from Woodcraft. Try to get a copy of this publication sheet if you can. You may have to buy a scraper.

Mounting the scrapers on magnets attached to the top cover is a good way to protect their edges.

Use the two upper drawers to hold the shavehooks, sanding blocks, Quick-Grip clamps, and the ubiquitous bits and pieces.

Using the Sanding and Gluing Workstation

You can use the sanding and gluing workstation for almost any operation where you need to clamp a workpiece. In addition to sanding and gluing, this includes drilling, routing, sawing, and any other work that requires the workpiece to be held or immobilized.

The drawers are clamping platforms. The height or width of the workpiece determines which drawer to use.

Clamping can be aided by using one of the 2x4 standoffs.

When the top drawers are used to hold the workpiece, the top face strip becomes the clamping bar.

The Quick-Grip hold-down clamps are ideal for clamping to the top of the station. Mounts for these clamps are located at each of the front corners. I find that I use the one on my left (facing the station) most of the time. If you plan on only one Quick-Grip hold-down, mount it on the left side.

When you are using doweling jigs like the Dowel Pro, clamping with the drawers allows the work to be held vertically. This is a far superior orientation than clamping the work on a horizontal surface.

Carcases like drawers and other box shapes can be set on the shelf. This shelf is also handy for setting tools and other items on as you are working. The advantage is that they are below the plane of the top and therefore out of the way.

With big, long boards, the extension table becomes a valuable accessory both for the station itself and, as I mentioned, for the saw.

Finally, the 2x4 standoffs can be used for clamping and gluing, either oriented as shown or rotated 90º.

The clamping standoffs are stored on the side of the workstation.

Plate Jointing

In addition to its other attributes, the sanding and gluing workstation is an ideal plate jointing station. The primary joints—butt, corner, surface and miter— are each readily accommodated. The station can both hold the work and act as a platform surface for the jointer. I use the Porter-Cable Model 555 jointer. It is equipped with a fence that is used to reference the cutter to the workpiece surface. For most cuts, I don't use this fence. Instead, I remove the fence and use the bottom of the jointer as the reference surface riding on top of the sanding and gluing workstation.

For corner and surface joints, one of the workpieces requires an end cut; for the butt joints, both pieces do. To make this cut, I clamp the workpiece to the station's top and, with the jointer riding the top surface, push the jointer into the workpiece.

For the corner cut, I clamp a board (normally one of the workpieces) to one of the clamping drawers, forming a fence at a right angle to the station's top. I clamp the workpiece to this auxiliary fence with the bottom edge resting on the station's top, then push the jointer into the workpiece to make the cut.

The surface joint is a variation of the corner joint, the difference being that the workpiece replaces the backing board. To position the workpiece so that it is level and normal to the station's top, I clamp a fram-

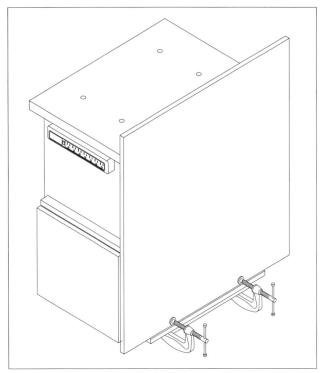

CLAMPING PANELS—LOWER DRAWER

ing square to the workpiece with the bottom leg of the framing square along the line where the mating piece will be positioned. Using the square's leg to hold the workpiece in its proper orientation, I clamp the workpiece to the clamping bar of the station's top. Next, I

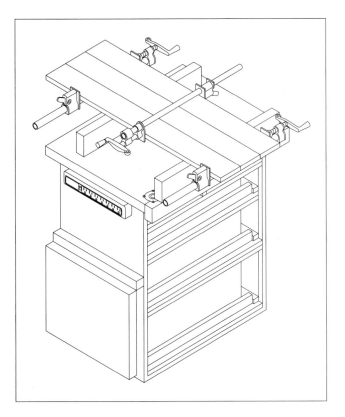

USING THE CLAMPING STANDOFFS
The clamping standoffs are 2x4s with dog pins (dowels) that secure them to the station's top. The standoffs allow the workpiece to be clamped from either side to minimize bowing. Note also the tray of water with the cloth and scrub brush for clean-up while the glue is still wet and manageable.

EXAMPLES OF PLATE JOINTING

Once you've marked the centers of the required cuts, it's a simple matter to clamp the workpiece and cut the butt or corner biscuit joints.

For the outside corners, position the vertical workpiece on the station's top. Use a backing board to support and clamp the workpiece as shown in the next picture.

The backing board clamps to the station in the same manner that a vertical workpiece is clamped to the station's clamping drawer.

For inside corner joints on the vertical piece, use a framing square to position the workpiece relative to the station's top. Use the backing board for additional support of the workpiece.

remove the framing square and proceed with the cutting as I did for the corner joint.

For the miter joints, I use the jointer in accordance with the manufacturer's instructions. If a large number of miter joints must be made, it's possible to either make a jig or raise the sanding and gluing workstation's top to the specified angle for holding the workpiece. Normally this is more trouble than it's worth.

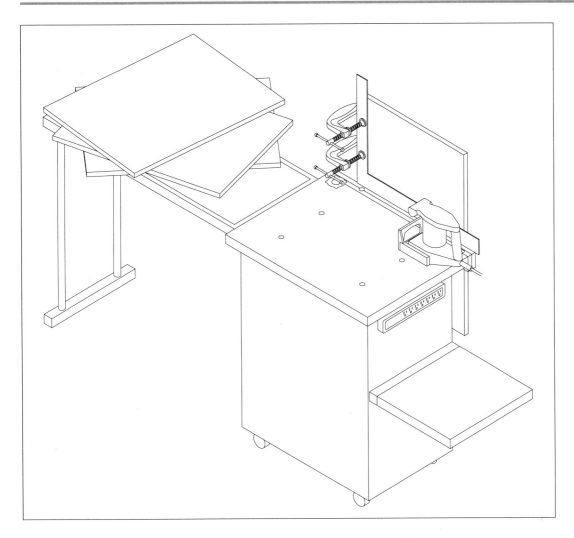

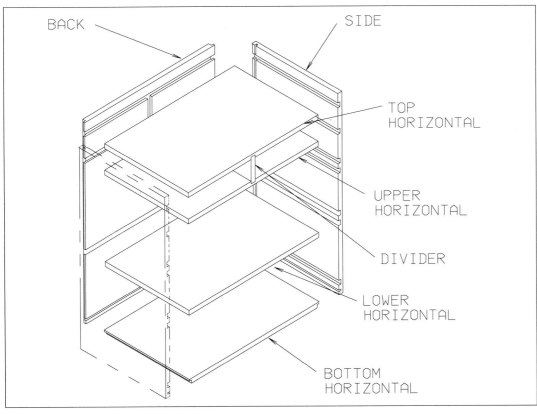

BACK

SIDE

TOP
HORIZONTAL

UPPER
HORIZONTAL

DIVIDER

LOWER
HORIZONTAL

BOTTOM
HORIZONTAL

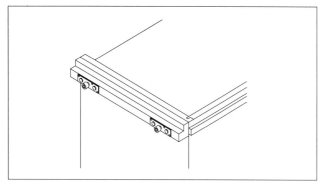

TOP AND EXTENSION TABLE MOUNTING

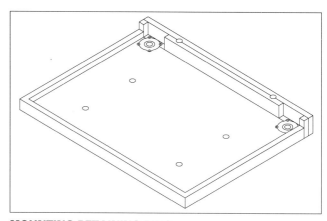

MOUNTING RETAINING RING

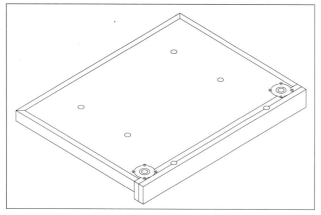

SANDING AND GLUING STATION TOP

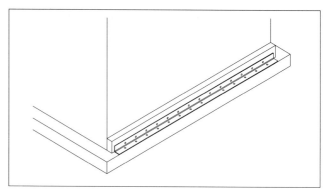

MOUNTING THE TOP

The adjustable tilt fence that comes with the Porter-Cable jointer works fine.

Building the Sanding and Gluing Workstation

The Carcase

Follow the procedures used for the other workstations when building the sanding and gluing workstation. The parts are assembled and glued as shown on page 107.

Once you've completed the basic carcase, make the pieces that are used to hold the drawers and to mount the top, shelf and extension table. The pieces used for mounting the top and the extension table look like this. The extension table attaches to the station with bed rail fasteners. (Woodworker's Supply PN. 823-962.)

The strips used as the drawer runner guides are cut to fit the previously cut dadoes and glued in place.

The top, shelf, drawer bases, and extension table are cut from a ¾" 4x4 sheet of 14-ply Baltic birch plywood trimmed with ¾" hardwood strips.

Building the Top

The finished top is shown above.

To mount the Quick-Grip Hold-Down retaining ring/flange, it will be necessary to cut away part of the inner top trim. This can be done before the inner strip is attached to the top, or after the trim is glued to the top. It must be done before the facing strip is glued to the inner trim strip. The bench dog holes are drilled after the top has been completed.

A piano hinge is used to mount the top to a spacer strip, which has been screwed and glued to the carcase. Note that the view shown here is upside down.

Building the Drawers

The two top drawers of the station are constructed in an identical manner as the drawers made for the table saw and the assembly stations. The lower drawers, designed as clamping platforms, are unique.

To build these drawers, first cut the bases from the ¾" 14-layer plywood. Next, cut the dado that is used to position the clamping bar, and then cut out the clamping access holes. Use a hole saw or large Forstner bit to cut the ends of the access holes. After

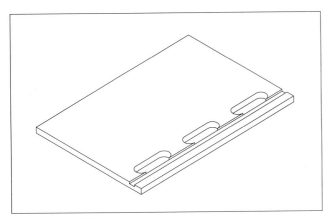

DRAWER BASE

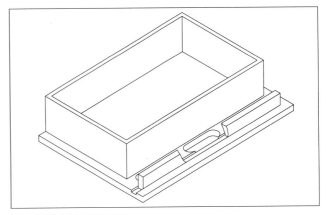

CLAMPING DRAWER

these holes have been cut or drilled, remove the remaining material using a saber saw. If necessary, the holes can then be cleaned up using a pattern bit in the router, followed by a round-over bit to smooth the edges.

Once you've completed the bases, attach the clamping bar to each base with glue and screws.

Build the drawers with any of the joints discussed, and glue-up as a subassembly before attaching, using glue and screws, to the drawer base. Make sure that the drawer box is square to the base and will not bind on the drawer rails attached to the case. You may want to attach the drawer box with screws to check the fit before gluing to the base.

Building and Mounting the Shelf

The side shelf, which is also cut from the 14-ply birch, is trimmed using hardwood strips and attached to the case with piano or strap hinges. A pair of table braces is used to hold the shelf in its "in use" horizontal position. The Stanley Drop Leaf 10" Table Brace, PN. 73-0550, works well for this application. These braces, sold in pairs, are carried by Woodworker's Supply under Woodworker's PN. 815-846.

Building the Extension Table

The last piece of the 4' x 4' x ¾" Baltic birch plywood is used to make the extension table. The table, of course, can be made larger than the one shown here. The size shown was a Hobson's choice—it was the amount of wood available from the 4x4 sheet.

This is a fold-up table that can be easily stored when not in use. There is always a proviso, and here

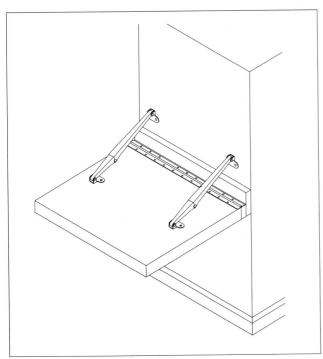

SHELF MOUNTING

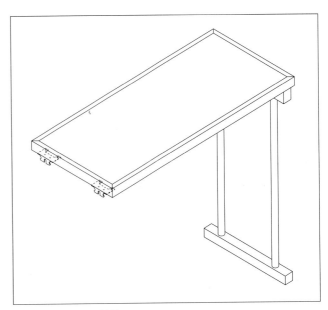

EXTENSION TABLE

LEG ASSEMBLY MOUNTING

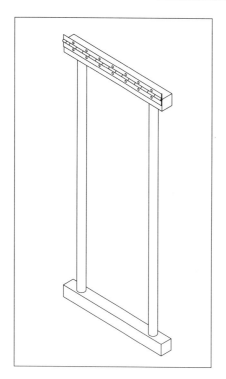

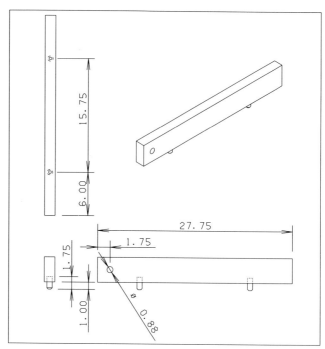

STANDOFFS

it's that you haven't added the drawer. The table attaches to the station with bed rail fasteners that are mounted horizontally, not vertically as they would be on a bed. The bed rails I've used are from Woodworker's Supply, PN. 823-962.

The basic table is constructed like a workstation top. It is surfaced with laminate and trimmed with hardwood. Its construction differs from a workstation top in that it is reinforced with 1½" by ¾" strips attached to the underside of the top behind the hardwood trim. These strips provide the mounting surface for the bed rails and the hinge for the folding legs.

The folding legs are 1" birch dowels mounted in hardwood stretcher bars. The top stretcher bar attaches to the reinforcing strip at the end of the table with piano or strap hinges as shown here.

Sanding and Gluing Workstation Accessories

The assembly workstation has no fixtures or accessories, and the sanding and gluing workstation has only a few: the standoffs, a sanding block(s), and a bench hook.

Standoffs

The standoffs are made from 2x4s. Try to find some good, dry straight studs when making these standoffs.

After you've made them, spend the extra time necessary to sand and finish them. When in use, they will constantly be covered with glue, and an oiled and finished surface is much easier to keep clean. Dry glue buildup can scratch workpiece surfaces as easily as 20-grit paper can.

It's also worthwhile to make a template for locating the peg holes and to use this same template for locating the holes in the station's top. If you err a little bit in locating these peg holes and the corresponding holes in the top, the bench dogs won't fit.

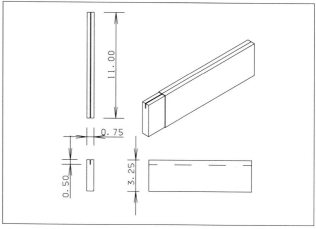

SANDING BLOCK

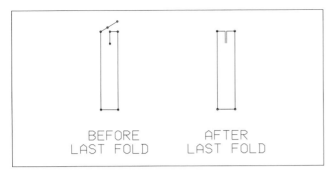

FOLDING THE SANDPAPER

Sanding Block

Everyone has a favorite sanding block design. This is mine. The same principle is used for holding the sandpaper in all of the size variations I use. They are all normally loaded with 100-grit paper because they are used to remove wood. They also can be used as finishing blocks, but finish sanding can be handled using a simple block wrapped with sandpaper.

All of the edges of the special block can be used, and in this sense it is used like a file. Once you are familiar with folding the paper and loading the block, you will find that it is worth the effort.

For the basic block, cut to the dimensions shown. The slot should be cut with a back saw or a panel saw. You want this slot just a little wider than the thickness of the folded sandpaper. The ⅛" kerf from the table saw is too wide.

To fold the paper, place one end in the slot, then using the block as the form, fold the paper around the block. Now crease the fold lines so that you have sharp corners. This will leave the last edge to be folded, the edge that doubles back; this edge, together with the first edge, will be positioned in the slot. Place this unfolded edge in the slot, fold it and then crease it. The diagram above shows the sandpaper before and after the last fold. To load, slide the folded paper onto the block.

When you get the knack of folding the paper, it will go quickly and the paper will be tight on the block.

One variation of this design is a block that is planed to a thickness of slightly less than ¾". With the paper in place, the block is ¾" thick and can be used to clean and widen dadoes. Other variations are shown and explained in the photograph at right.

Bench Hook

The bench hook allows you to saw, drill and cut without marring the station's top. This design has been around ever since the first bench was built. I planned the dimensions for this bench hook so it can sit on the table and the table's drawer can be opened. The hook is narrow enough to be stored between the table's legs when it is not being used. Shooting boards and other aids for the station should be made the same way, that is, plan where you want to put it and then cut it to a size that will fit the function and location you have chosen.

Vise

There will be times when you will want a regular vise at the station. I keep two vises on one of the power tool benches. Each has bench hooks mounted to its base for use with the sanding and gluing station. I also use a Bessey clamp-on bench vise with the station.

SANDING BLOCKS
The basic sanding block is a piece of ¾" stock cut to hold a full piece of sandpaper. Variations shown here include a piece of ¾" stock planed so that the resultant thickness of the block plus sandpaper is ¾". This block can be used to clean and enlarge ¾" dadoes.

Two other blocks are shown. One holds ¼ sheet of sandpaper; the other is a sanding stick that is used like a file. Note that the sanding stick is longer than the sandpaper. When one end is worn out, slide the paper to the other end and keep sanding.

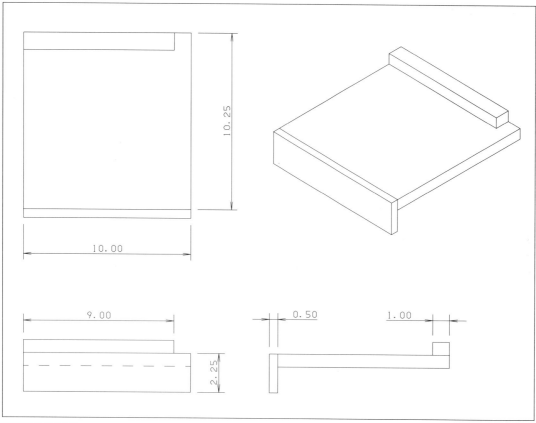

BENCH HOOK

VISES

Vises mounted on bench hooks can be brought to the station when needed. If necessary the bench hook bases can be clamped to the table, though this is normally not required. Also shown here is the normal bench hook and the Bessey clamp-on bench vise. This particular vise can be stored in either of the station's top drawers.

Drawings, Cutting List and Materials List

CUTTING LIST Carcase—See Cutting Diagram

PART	QTY	DESCRIPTION	MATERIAL	COMMENTS
Back	1	31.13" x 24.00" (31⅛" x 24")	¾" Shop Birch	
Side	2	31.13" x 16.00" (30⅛" x 16")	¾" Shop Birch	Right and Left
Horizontals	4	24.00" x 15.63" (24" x 15⅝")	¾" Shop Birch	
Divider	1	15.25" x 4.13" (15¼" x 4⅛")	¾" Shop Birch	
Runners	8	¾" x 1" x required length (cut to fit)	Hardwood	Drawer supports
Trim	—	¾" x ¾" border trim. Approximately 3' x 8"— Same material will be used for drawer pulls and other trims.	Hardwood	Pick wood color desired—contrasting or blending.

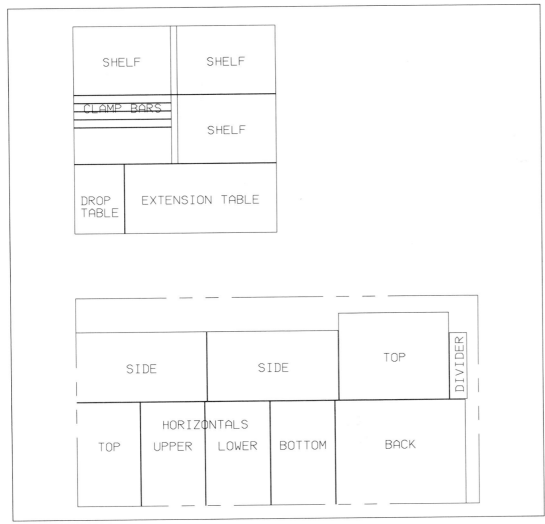

CUTTING DIAGRAM

HARDWARE

PART	QTY	DESCRIPTION	SOURCE	COMMENTS
Wheels	2	Casters, 2 " swivel	Woodworker's Supply PN. 812-958	
Wheels	2	Casters, 2 " fixed	Woodworker's Supply PN. 813-462	
Piano Hinge, brass	1		Woodworker's Supply Part No. 100-041	
Power Strip	1	7–15 amp, 125 V grounded outlets.		
Bed Rail Fastener	1 set		Woodworker's Supply PN. 823-962	
Drop-leaf shelf support	1 pair	10" supports	Woodworker's Supply PN. 815-846	
Quick-Grip Hold-Down	2	Bench clamps	Woodworker's Supply PN. 826-886	
Magnets	4	¾" round	Woodworker's Supply PN. 814-666	

BACK

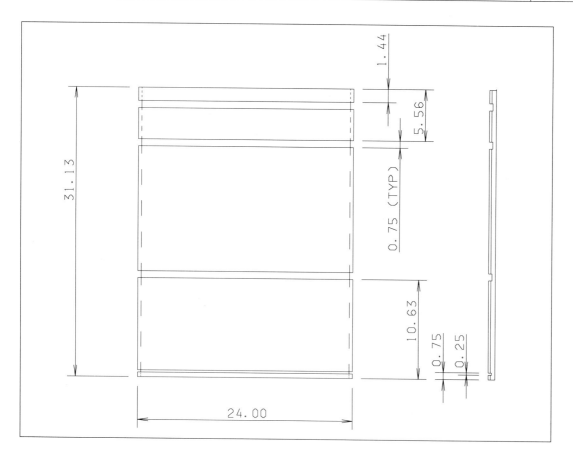

DRAWERS

PART	QTY	DESCRIPTION	MATERIAL	COMMENTS
Top Drawer	2			
Front/Back	2	11.25" x 3.38" (11¼" x 3⅜")	½" Baltic birch plywood	
Side	2	15.25" x 3.38" (15¼" x 3⅜")	¼" 5 layer plywood	
Bottom	1	11" x 15"	⅛" hardboard	
Top Clamp Drawer	1			
Front/Back	2	4.50" x 21.13" (4½" x 21⅛")	½" Baltic birch plywood	
Side	2	4.50" x 12.38" (4½" x 12⅜")	¼" 5 layer plywood	
Bottom	1	23.25" x 15.88" (23¼" x 15⅞")	¾" Baltic birch plywood	
Center Clamp Drawer	1			
Front/Back	2	7.19" x 21.13" (7³⁄₁₆" x 21⅛")	½" Baltic birch plywood	
Side	2	7.19" x 12.38" (7³⁄₁₆" x 12⅜")	½" Baltic birch plywood	
Bottom	1	23.25" x 15.88" (23¼" x 15⅞")	¾" Baltic birch plywood	
Lower Clamp Drawer	1			
Front/Back	2	9.13" x 21.13" (9⅛" x 21⅛")	½" Baltic birch plywood	
Side	2	9.13" x 12.38" (9⅛" x 12⅜")	½" Baltic birch plywood	
Bottom	1	23.25" x 15.88" (23¼" x 15⅞")	¾" Baltic birch plywood	
Clamp Bar	3	21.13" x 1.75" (21⅛" x 1¾")	¾" Baltic birch plywood	
Drawer Pulls	2	1.50" x 23.00" (1½" x 23")	1" (¾") hardwood	Pick wood color desired—contrasting or blending.

TOP

PART	QTY	DESCRIPTION	MATERIAL	COMMENTS
Base	1	26.25" x 20.00" (26¼" x 20")	¾" Shop Birch	See section on "Workstation Tops," page 16.
Borders	—	1.5" x 100.0" (1½" x 100")	¾" hardwood	Pick wood color desired—contrasting or blending.
Top Surface	1	26.75" x 20.50" (26¾" x 20½")		See section on "Workstation Tops," page 16.

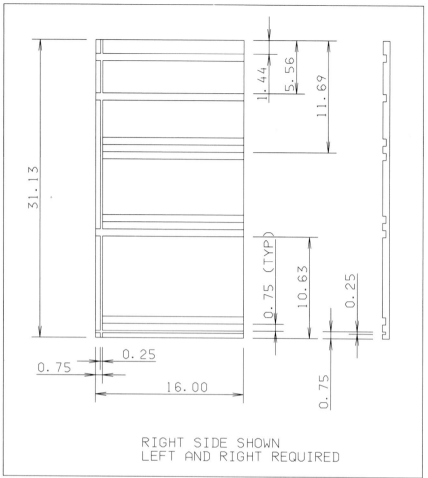

RIGHT SIDE SHOWN
LEFT AND RIGHT REQUIRED

SIDES

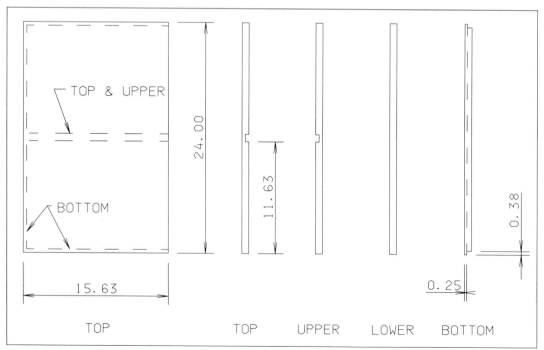

TOP & UPPER

BOTTOM

TOP   TOP   UPPER   LOWER   BOTTOM

HORIZONTALS

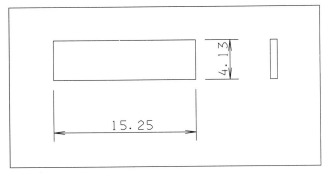

DIVIDERS

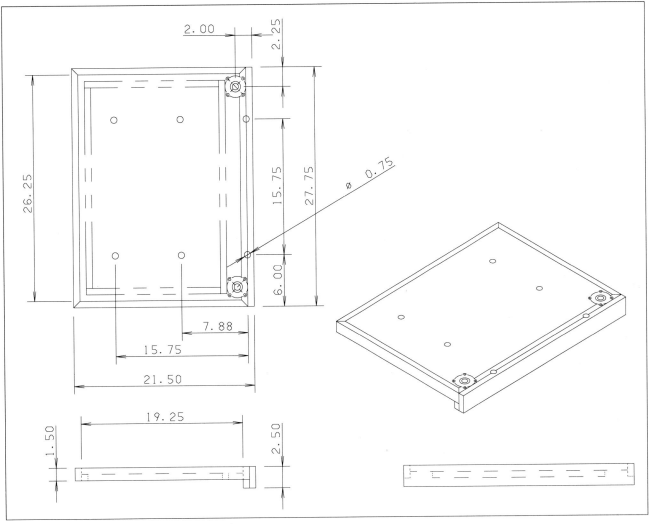

TOP

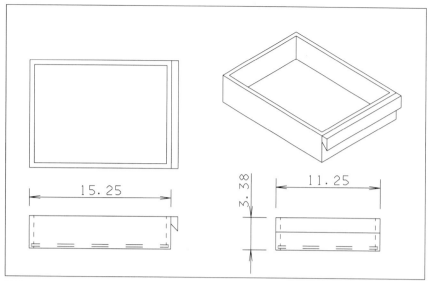

TOP DRAWERS

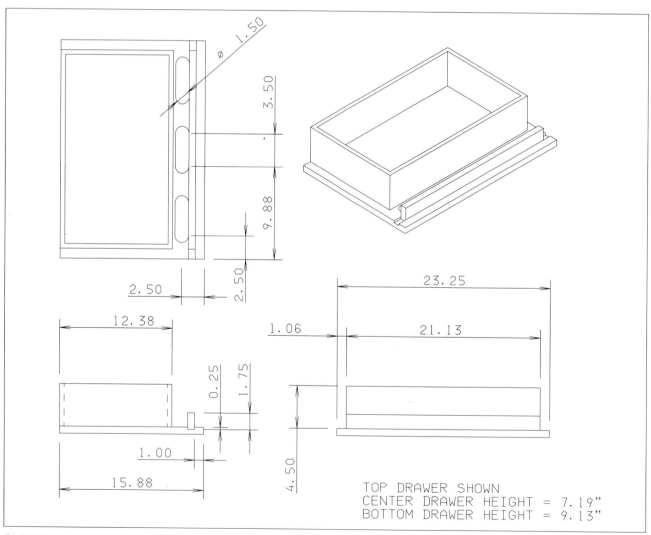

TOP DRAWER SHOWN
CENTER DRAWER HEIGHT = 7.19"
BOTTOM DRAWER HEIGHT = 9.13"

CLAMPING DRAWERS

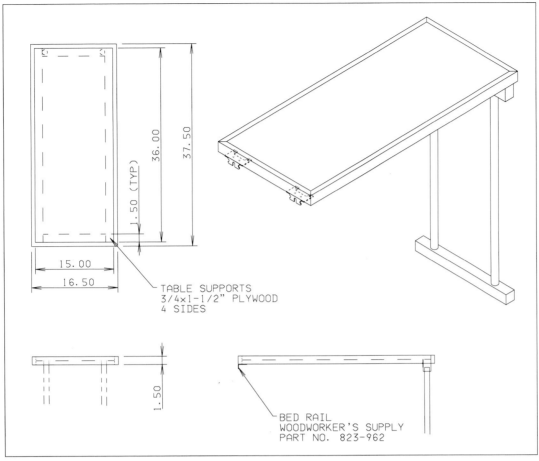

TABLE SUPPORTS
3/4×1-1/2" PLYWOOD
4 SIDES

15.00

16.50

36.00

37.50

1.50 (TYP)

1.50

BED RAIL
WOODWORKER'S SUPPLY
PART NO. 823-962

EXTENSION TABLE

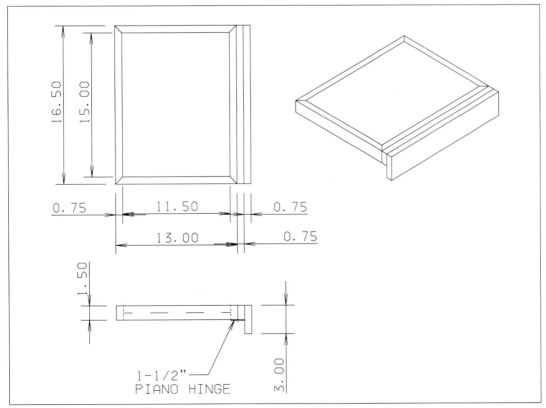

16.50

15.00

0.75

11.50

0.75

13.00

0.75

1.50

1-1/2"
PIANO HINGE

3.00

DROP SHELF

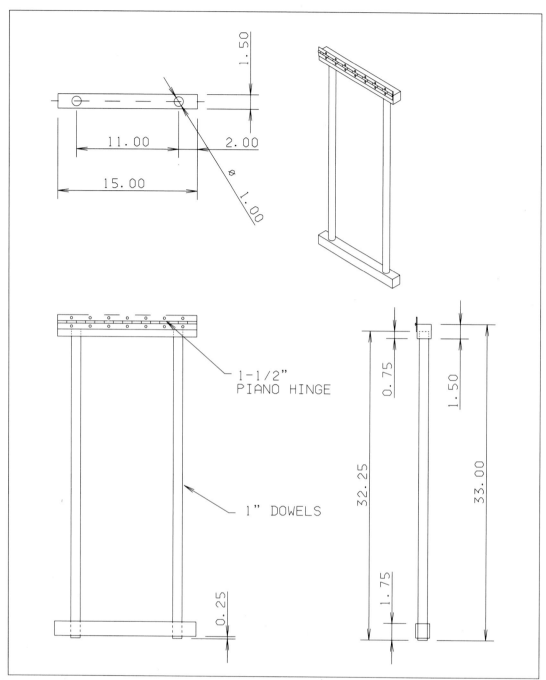

1-1/2"
PIANO HINGE

1" DOWELS

15.00

11.00

2.00

φ 1.00

1.50

0.75

1.50

32.25

33.00

1.75

0.25

EXTENSION TABLE LEGS

CHAPTER FIVE

THE POWER TOOL BENCHES AND RELATED STORAGE

CLOSED STATIONS

This version of the power tool bench is on wheels. The bench top holds frequently used benchtop tools. These tools can be removed and replaced with the scroll saw or bench grinder that are stored on the shelf above the bench. Also shown above and behind the bench are cabinets for holding supplies. These cabinets are accessible by reaching around the power tools. When an additional worktable is needed, the bench is rolled out and the tools placed on the garage floor.

Your workstations, all of the leftover wood, and all of that "other stuff" need to be stored somewhere.

Where can you put it so you can find it and get it easily when you need it? Where can you find storage for the 80 percent of the things you have but you use far less than 20 percent of the time? Some things are being used all the time, and others are never used.

The things that are never used but are much too "neat" or valuable to throw away must be stored. It is also necessary to store that which is not amenable to storage, such as, for example, wood.

In this chapter we will look at some ways to solve these storage problems.

The Power Tool Benches

The power tool benches are the parking structure for the workstations as well as a surface for holding your tabletop bench tools.

Closed and Open Workstations

The accompanying picture depicts the stations in their "closed" configuration, when the stations are parked. The "open" configuration is when the stations are out and in use.

In the closed or put-away configuration, the workstations are stored under a double bench. This bench is called the power tool bench and, as the name implies, is a place for the small benchtop power tools that are found in most home shops.

These benchtop tools are best mounted to their own subbases and not to the bench. If they are not permanently fastened, they can be mounted by their subbase to any of the workstations for use or moved to the workstations or placed under the bench to free up the work surface for other work.

Using a workstation as a tool stand gives you more working space and moves the heavy dust- and chip-producing work to the open area.

Benches can be built in one of two ways. The first way is to orient the workstations as shown in the above picture. The other is to orient them so that their drawers face outward; this orientation makes the drawers accessible even when the stations are in their "closed" position. The available space will dictate which orientation is best: short and fat or long and thin. I use both configurations.

Opening the workstations means pulling one or more of them out into the open area. You will normally start by pulling out the one that you need. At the end of the day they are all out. You may feel like a switching engine in a busy freight yard with all of the workstations out (and sometimes in the way), but that is the beauty of wheels. Give the stations a nudge and they are out of the way. (When doing your cha-cha with the workstations, however, remember that the wood leaning against them doesn't have wheels.)

If you look around and see that all of your compartments and tool holders are empty and you can't find an open surface anywhere, you'll know it's time to stop cutting and start putting your tools back where they belong.

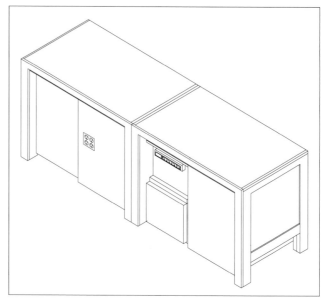

CLOSED STATIONS

When space is a problem, stations not being used are rolled back under the power tool benches.

Building the Power Tool Benches

Before the building can begin, some decisions must be made. First is the question of orientation. Should the workstation drawers face out or to the side? What is the length and width of the space that will be used for the power tool benches? Should the benches be on wheels? Or should the bench be hard-mounted to the wall?

The outline drawings presented here are for the minimum height and width of the inside opening for the short and fat configuration. Wheels can easily be added at any time. Merely cut the legs to account for the height of the wheel. A 3" wheel is best. One of the reasons for building the deeper bench is that there is room for some form of cabinets above and behind the bench and still enough bench top depth for the power bench tools. Another reason for the deeper bench is that, when the workstation sides are used to hold tools and fixtures, there is still room for the stations to roll under the bench. If space permits, the best solution can be to make the power tool benches wide enough and deep enough to accept the workstations in either orientation.

Whatever the orientation you choose, if the bench is to be hard-mounted to a wall, the construction can be simplified. The bench back is not required since its

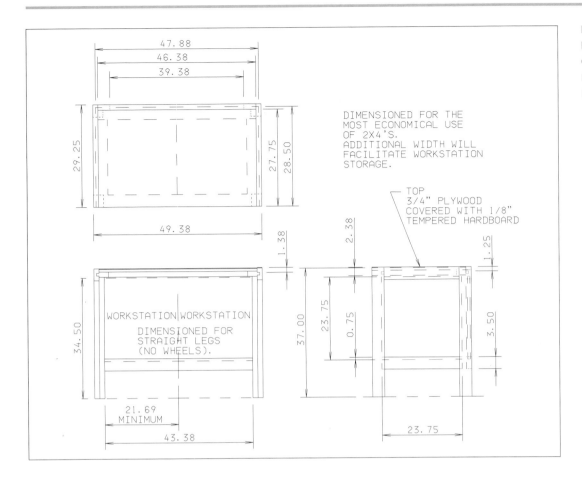

Building the Frame Panels

For the plans given, the benches are constructed with 2x4s and inexpensive ¾" plywood. The sides and the back are formed as panels that are joined to a top frame. This top frame is then covered with a sheet of the ¾" plywood, which in turn is covered with a sheet of tempered hardboard and trimmed with hardwood strips. This hardboard can be bonded to the plywood sheet with contact cement or tacked on.

The method of building the side is shown on page 124. A filler strip fills the dado in the leg bottom. The back is constructed in a similar manner.

The dadoes can be cut in the 2x4s before or after they have been cut to length. Normally, it is easier to cut the 2x4s first and then cut the dadoes. You will have more control of the workpiece when you work with the shorter lengths.

Glue and clamp the pieces together, including the filler block, making sure you check the square and the dimensions of the clamped assembly. Follow this procedure for both sides and the back.

Now cut the dado for the top. Use your router for this operation. Make the subtop frame in a similar manner to that of the sides and back.

Cut the leg supports from 2x4s and then glue, clamp and screw the parts together.

Building the Top

Construction of the top of the power tool benches is similar to that of the workstation tops. Tempered hardboard is used for the top laminate. The top is attached to the frame with screws that fasten from the underside.

It all comes together as shown on page 124. The top, which is not shown in the picture, rests on and attaches to the top frame.

The Wood Storage Rack

Unless you have an area dedicated to wood storage in your shop, finding a place to store your leftover wood will always present a problem. Even in commercial shops, the wood always takes more space than they want it to, and it is usually hard to get at.

Smaller shops, like the garage workshop, usually bring in what they need for the order and then cut

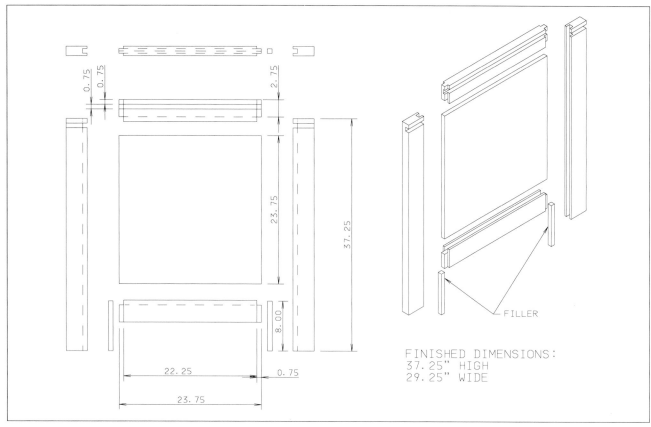

0.75
0.75
2.75
23.75
37.25
8.00
22.25
0.75
23.75

FILLER

FINISHED DIMENSIONS:
37.25" HIGH
29.25" WIDE

SIDE AND BACK CONSTRUCTION

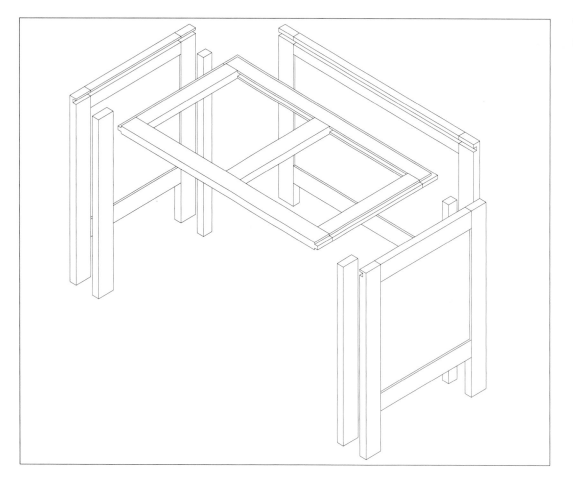

TOP ASSEMBLY

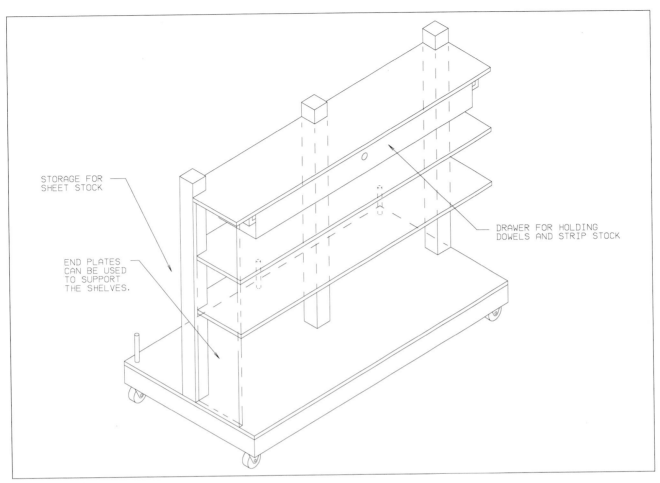

STORAGE FOR
SHEET STOCK

END PLATES
CAN BE USED
TO SUPPORT
THE SHELVES.

DRAWER FOR HOLDING
DOWELS AND STRIP STOCK

WOOD STORAGE CART

and mark the pieces as soon as possible. Sooner or later—usually sooner—the remnant pieces start collecting. In the garage workshop, they start collecting in the rafters, on the benchtops and in every corner. The best answer I know is to find something to make with these pieces. The only problem here is that you will invariably end up buying more wood to complete the new project and then find yourself looking for a place to store the *new* remnant pieces.

What I did was to build a cart that would hold most of the leftovers. When I had filled the cart I would start throwing away or building. My grandchildren have quite a collection of boats and planes as a result.

Constructing the Wood Storage Rack

The rack is shown in the following figure and picture. It has space for a reasonable amount of sheet stock, stock that started out as 4x8 sheets, a drawer for dowels, and shelves for lumber, cutoffs and odd pieces. On the bottom shelf are the cardboard boxes where I store the small cutoffs. End plates, like bookcase

sides, can be used to support the shelves. The disadvantage will be that pieces longer than the cart cannot be stored.

When I'm working, I normally roll the cart out onto the driveway. If there's rain or cold weather, the cart shares the warm space with me.

Use inexpensive material to build this cart and try to use as many of the pieces lying around as possible. I tried to save money on the casters, but that was a mistake. This cart with its load of wood is heavy. You want it to roll easily, so it needs good large casters.

The inverted T-section frame is constructed from 2x4s. The shelves and the end plates or sides are made from medium-density fiberboard (MDF) or ¾" plywood. The shelves can be mounted with right-angle, heavy-duty shelf brackets, 2x4 braces or end plates.

Using 2x4s instead of 4x4s for the T-section is cheaper, and they are easier to work with. Yards and home improvement centers often have sales on 2x4s but hardly ever on 4x4s. The joints are lap and a lazy man's mortise and tenons.

The cart initially didn't have a full bottom or a full divider between the shelves and the side where the sheet stock cutoffs are stored. This caused a problem with wood falling off and getting mixed with other wood. When possible I segregated the wood type, that is, oak, maple, birch, etc. To keep the sheet stock in place, I used ¾" dowels as shown in the detailed plans.

This cart works well if you have the space to store it. My garage is deep enough for the cart and a car. The cart could be stored outside with a tarp over it.

The dowel drawer slides on ¾" x ¾" runners. Using ½" stock for the drawer and the dimensions shown for

WOOD STORAGE CART

One side of the wood storage cart is used for storing the large remnants of the sheet stock. The far side is used for storing the smaller cutoffs, dowels and board stock.

The 2x4s attached at each end are the braces used for adapting the cart to a panel saw configuration.

WOOD STORAGE CART

To use the cart as a panel saw, the sheet stock must be removed. Note that the slots in the 2x4s are notched so they will remain up and out of the way without being clamped in place.

The panel saw guide can be seen stored on the garage door. It's not too heavy and is too long to be stored easily any other place. The guide can be removed from its holders with the door either in the up or down position.

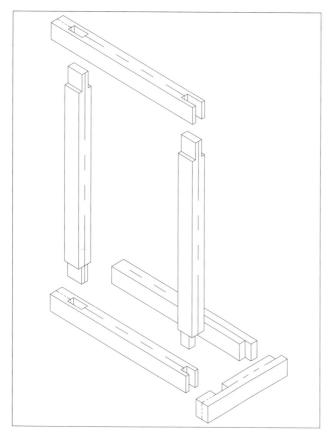

EXAMPLES OF JOINTS USED

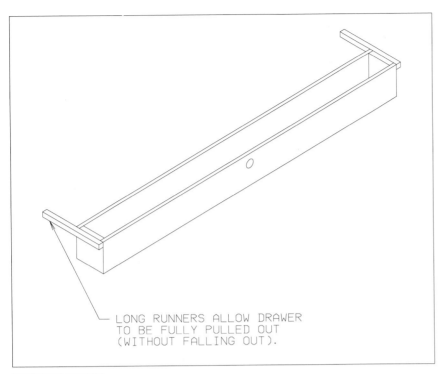

LONG RUNNERS ALLOW DRAWER
TO BE FULLY PULLED OUT
(WITHOUT FALLING OUT).

DRAWER DETAIL

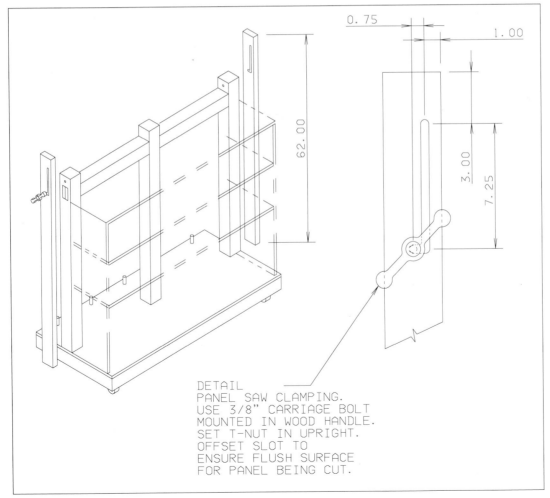

0.75

1.00

62.00

3.00

7.25

DETAIL
PANEL SAW CLAMPING.
USE 3/8" CARRIAGE BOLT
MOUNTED IN WOOD HANDLE.
SET T-NUT IN UPRIGHT.
OFFSET SLOT TO
ENSURE FLUSH SURFACE
FOR PANEL BEING CUT.

PANEL SAW SUPPORT

PANEL SAW
The panel saw guide is a large T square with a ¾" guide/rest. This guide/rest keeps the whole guide from bowing. Its top edge, which was cut with the panel saw, is the cut line and is aligned with the cut line on the sheet to be cut.

Sheet stock can be oriented vertically for cutting, but it is an awkward setup and not recommended for thin stock.

the basic cart width, you can keep 48" dowels in the drawer. If you downscale the cart, try to keep the drawer wide enough for 36" dowels. The drawer should be only 4½" to 5" deep. This depth allows the drawer to be pulled out without falling out. The runners are 10" long.

Panel Saw

Once you have a wood storage rack, it's a simple matter to add the provisions for cutting 4x8 sheet stock. A couple of 2x4s and a 9' length of 1x8 pine are all that you need. The 2x4s are cut as shown in the figure on page 127. They mount to the rack's uprights with ⅜" carriage bolts.

When not in use they remain attached to the uprights. When used they are rotated forward and lowered to support the sheet stock for cutting.

The guide for your circular saw is made from pine board into a large T square. One end is fixed and the other can be made adjustable from between 4' to 8'. The guide posed a storage problem until I ended up mounting it on the garage door. I now can get at it easily with the door either up or down.

Clamp Storage

The relatively new Quick-Grip clamps are easy to store because of their shape. This is not the case with pipe clamps, especially long pipe clamps. For these long

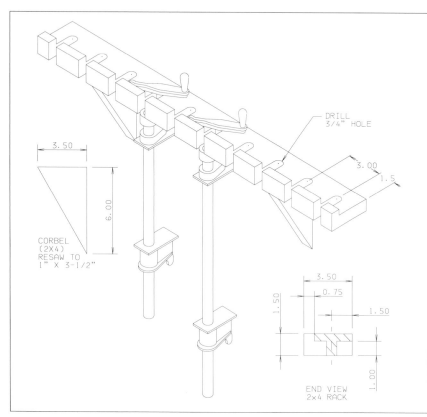

3.50

6.00

CORBEL
(2X4)
RESAW TO
1" X 3-1/2"

DRILL
3/4" HOLE

3.00

1.5

3.50

0.75

1.50

1.50

1.00

END VIEW
2x4 RACK

PIPE CLAMP RACK

clamps, a simple yet practical rack can be made from a 2x4.

1. Cut the 2x4 to the required length. The pipes hang on 3" centers, so a 30" length will allow you to hang 10 clamps.
2. Resaw the board, forming the lip that will retain the clamps.
3. Drill the ¼" holes on a line 2" back from the front edge.
4. Cut out the material between the holes and the front of the rack.

The best way to mount the rack to a wall is to make a pair of corbels, again from a 2x4, that attach to the rack and the wall. Resaw the corbels to a thickness of 1" so they won't interfere with the clamps, then position them between the second and third holes from each end. I have my rack mounted quite high (about 6" from the ceiling) so the long clamps can hang freely. This mounting for the long clamps is shown here.

Shop Layout

Rome wasn't built in a day, and neither will your shop be, but if you don't want it laid out like the streets of Rome, it will help to have a plan. A scaled floor plan is the best starting point. Identify the available space and what space you will need for your shop area. There is never enough space, so now is the time to see how you can consolidate some of your storage needs.

You will find that models help in this space planning. Using a scale of ⅒" = 1" works well for the models. A 36"-high table will be 3.6" high. Your floor plan should have a scale of something like 1/16" = 1". This scale also works well for smaller models, but it is harder to calculate the scale dimension.

EXAMPLE OF STORING PIPE CLAMPS
Long pipe clamps can be stored up high and away in a corner using the simple 2x4 pipe clamp rack. The one shown here is mounted to a garage joist. The long Quick-Grip type clamps hang from a clothespole rack.

RELATED JIGS AND FIXTURES

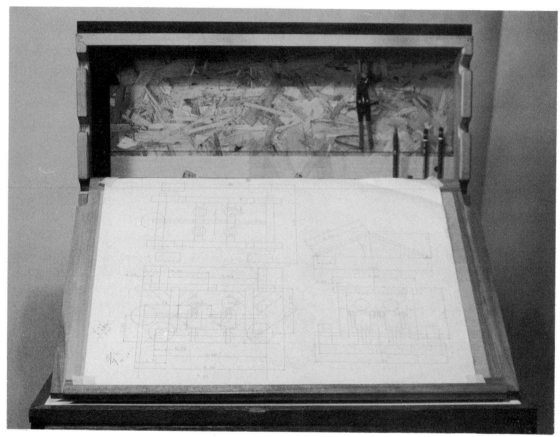

THE DRAFTING MODULE
The drafting module can sit on a workstation or on a power bench. Its case dimensions are that of a drawer, which allows it to be stored in an assembly-type workstation. The drafting board can also be removed and laid flat on any convenient surface.

You have built the four workstations and a number of jigs and fixtures you will be using in your woodworking projects. With these resources you are ready to tackle some meaningful work for your home and friends. But before starting these projects, you may want to tackle two more valuable aids for your shop.

These are the drafting module—a self-contained drafting board that fits as a drawer in one of your workstations—and a unique fence system for your router table.

The Drafting Module

A finished piece reflects the steps taken in its construction. To complete the construction you will need a plan. Whether it's a sketch or a detailed drawing, some form of the final design on paper is the best starting point. Use the drafting module to help you create this starting point.

The design here is for a drafting module that is stored as a drawer in an assembly-style workstation.

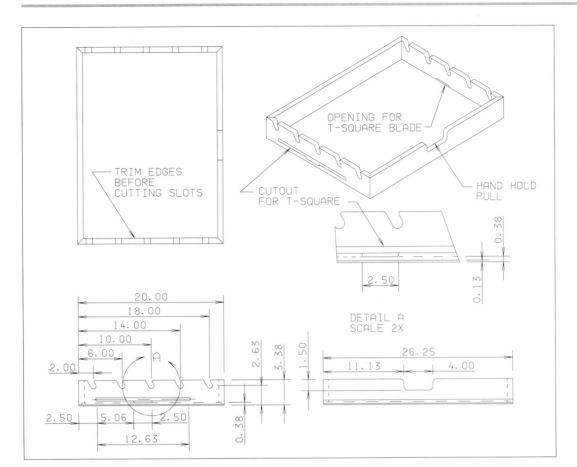

DRAFTING MODULE CASE
When selecting the T square, pick one that will require a minimum of trimming to fit the case.

When removed it can be set on a workstation or on a power bench. Put it where it is both out of the way and handy. I normally have mine on a power tool bench because I like the height and I also have a place for my knees. When I want the plans close to where I am working, I put the drafting module, or just the board, on one of the workstations.

Constructing the Drafting Module

Start by making the case box that will be the drawer holding the drafting board and your drafting tools. You should have some remnant shop birch pieces that can be used for this box.

Any of the corner joints I've discussed will work. Using a router cutter, I normally use a lock miter joint for this type of construction. The lock miter joint can also be cut using the saw, but that entails a number of steps and some accurate cutting. A diagonal splined miter also works well and is much simpler to make. I use my 45° vertical miter box to cut this type of joint, as shown in the following photograph.

The notches in the frame should be made by first drilling the holes and then, using either a band saw or a saber saw, cutting out the openings. Trim the edges

CUTTING DIAGONAL SPLINED MITERS
Making 45° cuts can be a bother. Cranking the blade to 45° and then back to 90° is time-consuming. A 45° jig that rides the fence like the tenon jig can minimize the bother and save time. To miter the ends of the drafting module sides, first cut the miters, then turn the workpiece over, reset the blade height and fence-to-blade distance, and make the spline cut.

Make sure the spline cut is at exactly the same distance from the workpiece end on all of the sides.

with hardwood before cutting these slots. I would also suggest taking the extra step and making a pattern for a pattern bit to finish the final shaping of the slots. Now cut the openings for the T square and rabbet the back edges. The back itself can be made from any number of materials. I have used hardboard, MDF, chipboard and plywood. The chipboard, when well sanded and finished with a gloss lacquer, has an interesting and attractive pattern.

Attach the two tool holders. The top holder is slotted to hold triangles and has holes to hold drafting pencils. The bottom holder is actually a rabbeted base for the pencils and triangles to rest on. A pull handle can be attached to the top of the case, or a cutout hand pull can be used in the base.

Making the Drafting Board

To make the drafting board, start by making a glue-up for the pivot block. Form the block by gluing two 1¼" x 24¾" lengths of ¾" stock to a 2½" x 24¾" piece of ¾" stock. Leave it this way until the board is completely assembled and glued and then round-over as shown in the drawing. Now cut the actual drafting board and border with hardwood. As shown I used a tongue-and-groove joint for joining the pivot block and the border to the board. Note that the trim border has a rabbeted edge that will rest on the module case. If you want to cover the board, now is the time. Vinyl is used most commonly and can be purchased locally or ordered from Dick Blick Art Materials, (800) 447-8192.

The drafting tools I used in this design came from Staedtler, Inc., P.O. Box 2196, Chatsworth CA 91313. Product No. 999 SS1—Student Drafting Kit. It con-

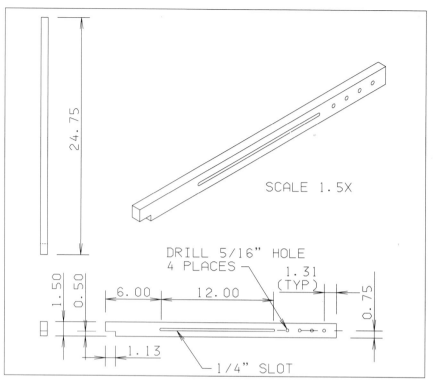

DRAFTING MODULE UPPER TOOL HOLDER

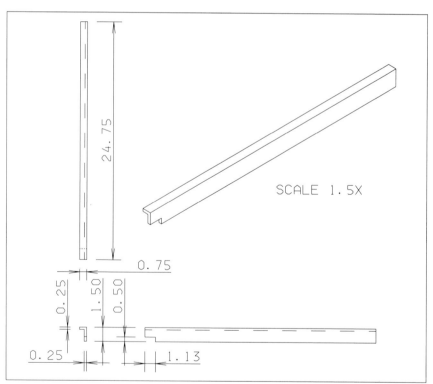

DRAFTING MODULE LOWER TOOL HOLDER

tains a T square, 30° triangle, 45° triangle, scale, compass and other miscellaneous pieces. For the T square to fit in the module (and in the workstation), it will be necessary to cut about ½" from both ends—another application of the Theorem of Procrustes.

DRAFTING MODULE TOOL HOLDER PLACEMENT

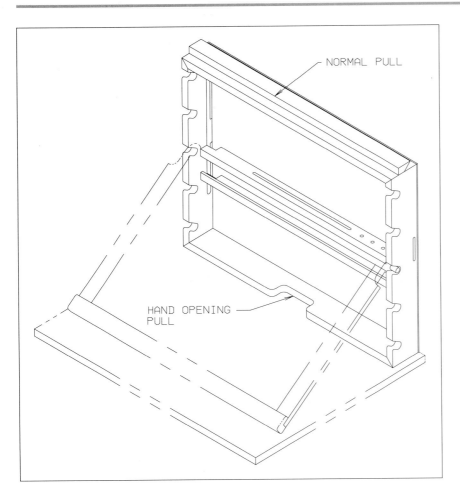

NORMAL PULL

HAND OPENING PULL

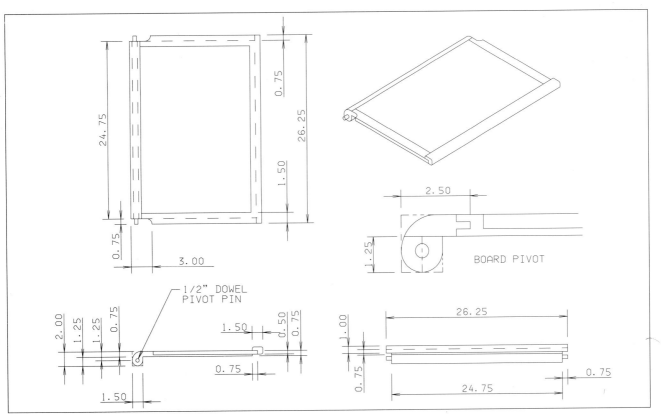

0.75

26.25

24.75

1.50

0.75

3.00

1/2" DOWEL PIVOT PIN

2.00

1.25

1.25

0.75

1.50

0.50

0.75

1.50

0.75

BOARD PIVOT

2.50

1.25

1.00

26.25

0.75

24.75

0.75

DRAFTING MODULE DRAWER

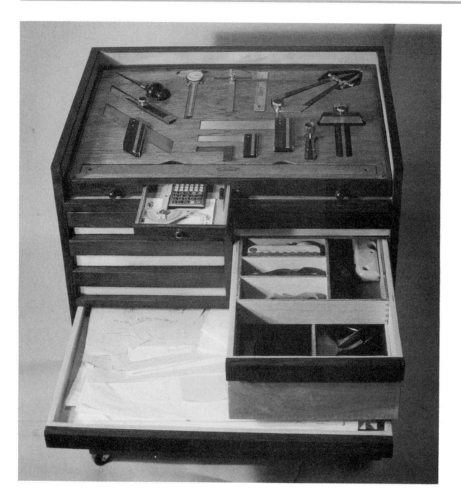

CUSTOM WORKSTATION

The custom workstation shown here holds the Bridge City Tool Works layout tools, a drawer of planes, the drafting module, a drawings tray, and a specially designed tool chest for miniature/hobby-class tools.

The other drawers are used for quality hand tools, sharpening stones, jigs and related items.

This workstation is normally rolled up to the sanding and gluing workstation and is used as a support station.

Drafting Module Workstation

An assembly-style workstation works well as a home for the drafting module. The one I have built for myself is shown above.

This workstation is far more than a home for the drafting module. The top slide-out tray/drawer holds my special layout and measuring tools. I own the Bridge City Tool Works "Square Deal Plus" set of tools and wanted to have them handy and also protected. It didn't seem right to let these beautiful, expensive tools bang together in a drawer. The tray that holds this set has a recessed cutout for each tool. This recess is deeper at the base end. When the tool's base is pressed down, the tool pivots up for removal. I also store the DC-40 Dividing Compass in this tray along with some layout and measuring tools I have always used: a small, 2" try square; a micrometer; and a scale and protractor. A small drawer built into the tray holds the accessory items that come with the DC-40 Dividing Compass, a unique protractor (which is also available from Bridge City Tools) and a calculator.

Below the tray are four standard-sized drawers and one double-sized drawer. The double-sized drawer, which has a lift-out tray, holds my planes. The jointer and jack planes were too wide to fit on their sides in a standard drawer.

The other drawers hold chisels, files and sharpening stones, and a set of carving knives. Below the drawers is a full width 1½"-high drawer for drawings. If you are going to be making drawings, you will need a place to keep them. I didn't use slides for this drawer because it is light and I wanted the full width of the station. I used ¼" plywood for the bottom to give the drawer strength. The drawer will hold C sized (17" x 22") drawings without folding.

Next is the space for the drafting module, and under the module is space for my hobby chest. This chest, like the drafting module, can be set up on a workstation, on a power tool bench, or if it will be used frequently, it can be hung on a wall.

The top of this workstation is a departure from the norm. It is 23" deep by 29¼" wide. This increased size offers a clamping ledge along the sides and front of the station. The clamping edges are primarily used with hobby-class tools or for holding layout or sharpening-type fixtures. The height is the standard 34½".

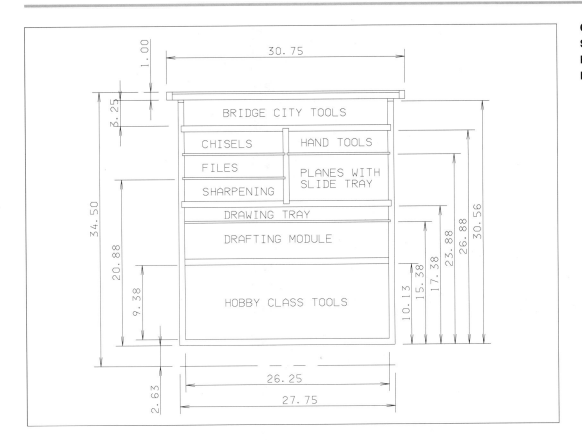

BRIDGE CITY TOOLS

CHISELS

HAND TOOLS

FILES

PLANES WITH SLIDE TRAY

SHARPENING

DRAWING TRAY

DRAFTING MODULE

HOBBY CLASS TOOLS

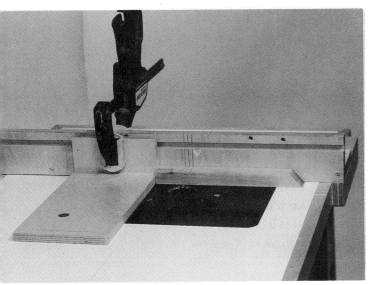

THE SLIDING FENCE

See top of page for front elevation of the workstation.

The Special Router Fence System

Measure once, cut twice. It sounds like heresy, but if you are going to be making repetitive cuts, you don't want to have to measure and layout the cut lines on each piece. The best solution is to do the layout once and then, using your fixtures, repeat this cut as many times as required. A saw miter with a stop is a good

example of this philosophy. Building the special fence system for your router workstation will let you make repeatable cuts after measuring once. Of course, there is a price to pay. Building the fence system will require some time, and you'll need to measure twice and cut once while you are building it—it's a one-time charge. When you've finished it, you'll know its value.

This fence system is in reality a number of jigs and fixtures built around the sliding fence. I built the sliding fence to solve a problem I was having in using a box joint. The problem was that I couldn't allow any accumulated tolerance to build up over the length of the workpiece. Using a normal box joint jig, the error in the jig's spacing resulted in 15 times the error over the length of the workpiece I was using. I needed the final pin to be an exact distance from the starting pin. To solve this need, I designed the sliding fence. Sliding on the router station's top, the fence could slide into the cutter bit, thereby marking exactly where the cut would be made on the fence's face. Using a pencil, I extended both sides of the cut lines to the top of the fence. These lines were then used to position the marked workpiece with respect to the cutter path. The asymmetrical position of the router with respect to the station's top allowed the fence to slide from right to left and left to right. This meant that two cutter positions could be located; in my case, this was one for a ½" cutter and one for a ¾" cutter.

One of the beauties of this setup is that, without any adjustment or measuring, the location of the cutter to the fence is fixed and known—that is, it is repeatable any time you use the fence. As I discussed in chapter two, the router-to-router plate relationship must remain fixed for this repeatability to be assured.

This repeatability allows a number of cutting operations to be done quickly and accurately. A right-angle stop was added so that duplicate cuts could be made on any number of workpieces—the bookcase example. An extension was then added for longer workpieces.

To accommodate miter cuts, an apron was added to the back side of the fence. To secure the workpiece for miter cuts, stops are tacked to the apron at the required angle. For some of the cutting operations, like cutting arcs, the fence got in the way, so I made a sliding fence without the fence. This fenceless fence is clamped to the workstation top to position the workpiece relative to the cutter. I use dowel pins for the pivot point. This setup is being used to cut the taper jig pivot arm in the example shown here. Use spacers to keep the workpiece level with the slide platform.

As I used the fence I continued adding new cutting fixtures and holders. The first was an extension stop that replaced the right-angle stop for longer workpieces. This extension stop, shown above right, is secured both by clamping and by fitting into a sliding dovetail cut in the fence's face. For extremely accurate positioning of both the right-angle stop and the extension stop, I developed the threaded adjustment locator. Using a 10-32 machine screw as the locator, adjustment to ⅟₁₂₈" is possible. As with most cuts, the exact dimension is not as important as the relative position of the cut to some baseline or a cut in a mating piece.

Next came the nudger. When the sliding fence is clamped to the router station's top, it becomes a normal fence. The nudger is used for accurate positioning of the fence to cutter distance. It can be clamped so that it nudges either the front of the fence or the rear of the fence. Using a cam-type design, it will accurately position the fence to within ⅟₆₄". A picture of the nudger is shown in chapter two with the knobs.

To make vertical cuts—for example, end cut dovetails in narrow stock—I needed a way to hold the workpiece in this vertical position. The answer was to build a sliding holder. The fence already had a dove-

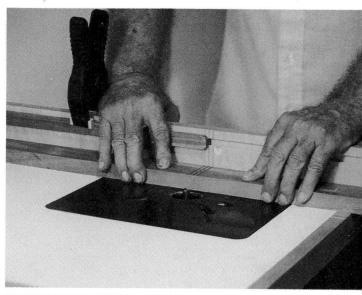

SLIDING FENCE—EXTENSION STOP
A variation of the sliding fence is this sliding platform used for miter cuts and cutting arcs.

CUTTING ARCS
The example shows the pivot arm of the saw's taper jig being cut. The drawn pattern of the arm is glued to the workpiece to aid in the cutting. Remember to cut from the outside in so you don't lose the pivot point. Also predrill the enlarged end holes, or at least the starting hole, for the internal arc. The enlarged starting hole will keep the router bit from grabbing when the router is turned on.

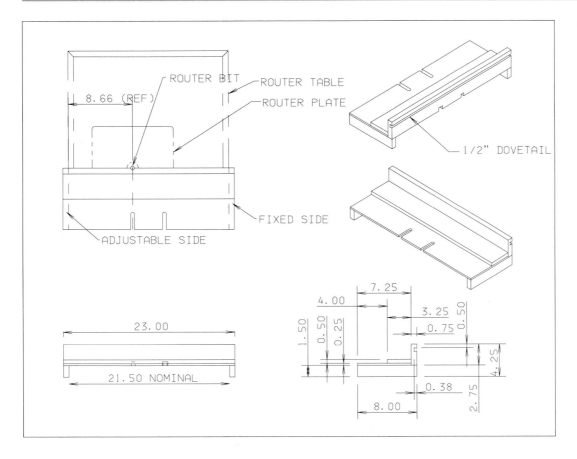

tail slot in its front face, and I used this slot to mount the vertical clamp.

Finally, I added the box joint jig. When one box is being made, this jig will cut the waste between the pins on both ends and sides at the same time. It will handle 4 pieces of up to ½" stock that is up to 6" wide. It handles ⅛" spacing and any multiple thereof.

Collectively, these fixtures and accessories constitute the special fence system. Start with the basic sliding fence and then plan on building the add-on tools as they are required.

Building the Sliding Fence

The basic fence is rather straightforward. Five pieces must be cut and assembled. For the fence system to work, your router station top must be a perfect rectangle. If it isn't, the sliding fence won't work as well as it should. Check your top and, if necessary, trim it so you have 4 right angles and 4 flat sides.

Cut the pieces for the fence and fasten first with screws only. Later you can glue the arm and the sub-base to the base. Make sure the base is at 90° to the top's side and that the fence face is at 90° to the station's top.

Put a ½" straight cutting bit in the router and set the fence on the tabletop. Turn on the router and slide the fence into the cutter enough to completely profile the cutter bit in the fence's face. Turn off the router and remove the fence. Now, using a pencil extend the bit profile to the top of the fence. At this time you may also want to mark the center of the cut. If, for example, you will be using a ¼" bit, the positioning of the workpiece will be with respect to the center, not the edge. Turn the fence around and make another cut in its face, this time with a ¾" bit. Extend the bit profile as before, and you have completed the basic sliding fence. You can add the dovetail slot at this time or later. I never permanently attach the fence to the base because I may want to modify it or replace it.

The Right-Angle Stop

Before using the sliding fence you need a stop, which is a simple right-angle fixture that is clamped in position. A box joint is probably the best joint for connecting the two pieces. Just make sure you've formed an exact right angle and that the resulting assembly is at a right angle to the fence face. To use the stop, position the marked workpiece against the fence, then slide the stop up to the workpiece's edge and clamp the stop to the fence. When sliding the workpiece

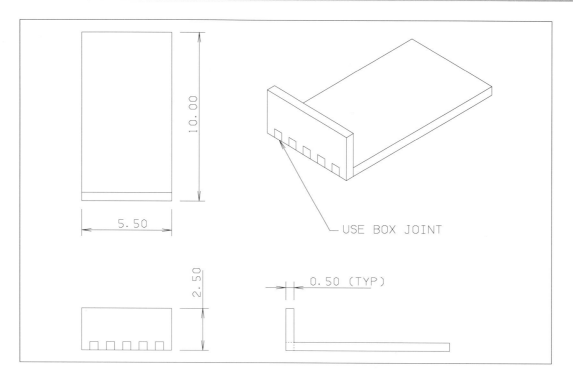

10.00

5.50

2.50

USE BOX JOINT

0.50 (TYP)

into the cutter, place your hands on the fence and use your fingers to hold the workpiece against both the fence and the stop. If you are making a cut at the edge of the workpiece, you will need to use a hold-down.

One of the nice features about the sliding fence is that, when you have completed the cut, the cutter bit is under the fence, protecting you and the workpiece. Never drag the fence back while the router is on and the workpiece is still positioned. Position the workpiece and the stop, turn the router on, and slide over the bit to make the cut. Then turn the router off and remove the workpiece, leaving the fence over the router bit.

The Extension Stop

To use the extension stop it will be necessary to cut a dovetail slot in the fence. Make the dovetail cuts in the extension stop bar at the same time. It is also a good idea to cut a number of bars at this time (you can also cut a longer bar). The extra length or pieces will be used for some of the other tools. By cutting them all now you have only one final setup to make. The fit of the sliding dovetail should be loose enough so that there is no binding; the bar should slide easily in the fence's dovetail slot. When cutting the dovetail bar stock, clamp the sliding fence to the top. Cut both sides, working toward the center by moving the fence, until you have the fit you want. Now cut the dado in the stop's arm and fasten to the bar. What you will

end up with is a small T-square. Pin the arm to the bar with ⅛" or 3⁄16" dowels Use the extension stop when the workpiece's edge-to-cutter distance is greater than the length of the fence.

The Threaded Adjustment Locator

Make the threaded adjustment locator from the extra bar stock that was previously cut. Drill a No. 10-32 tap hole and cut the tap. If you don't have the drill and tap, you can use an insert, like when you make a knob. Thread a 10-32 machine screw into the block and put two nuts at the end of the screw.

To use the adjustment locator, clamp it next to the stop and turn the screw until the nut is touching the stop. Now move the stop and turn the screw (fore or aft) until you have the adjustment you want to make. This adjustment is determined by the amount the initial cut in the workpiece or scrap was off from the planned cut. Each complete revolution of the screw is 1⁄32" displacement. A half turn is 1⁄64" and a quarter turn is 1⁄128" of horizontal change.

The Nudger

You can make the adjuster for the nudger like the threaded adjustment locator, or you can do as I have done and cut a cam for this adjustment. The best way I have found to make the cam is to lay it out on paper and then paste the layout on the piece of wood that will become the cam. Write the distances on the lay-

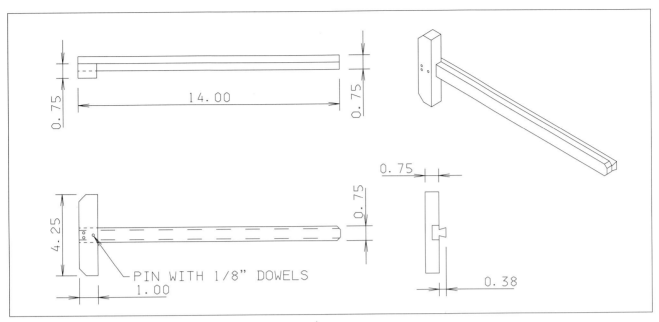

EXTENSION STOP

out so the marked distances label the cam. Drill the pivot hole and rough cut the cam, making sure you stay outside the lines that represent the cam faces. Using a 1" belt sander, sand each face to the face line.

Use the nudger the same way you use the threaded adjustment locator. Have the zero face against the fence and clamp it to the top. Now move the fence and turn the cam to the required adjustment (plus or minus), move the fence back until it touches the cam face, and then clamp the fence to the top.

Most of the time when you use the sliding fence you won't need the adjusters. When you do need them, you will have them.

The Box Joint Jig

Setting up to do box joints on the router can be time-consuming. As with most cutting, it never takes long to make the actual cut. What takes time is measuring and setting up to make the cut. I wanted an accurate and fast way to make box joints for one box, cutting the sides and the ends at the same time, so I designed this jig. If I have multiple boxes to make, I use the box joint jig on the saw. I also wanted to be able to make the box joints on the router so that the saw was free for cutting and I didn't have to bother with loading and unloading the dado blades.

The two problems I have experienced most often

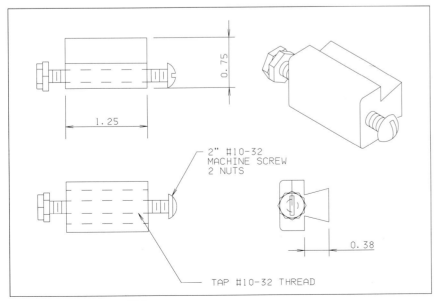

ADJUSTMENT LOCATOR

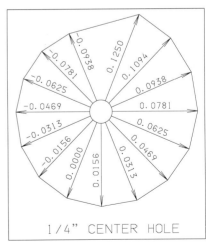

NUDGER CAM

NUDGER CAM

1/4" CARRIAGE BOLT WITH STAR KNOB

2.25

15.25

22.00

4.00

1.75

2.00

9.75

2.00

3.00

1.00

2.25

6.00

2.00

with any box joint jig are keeping the workpiece vertical and clamping close to the cutter. This box joint jig solves both of those problems. It uses the sliding fence, so there is a known and repeatable reference with respect to the cutter. To use the jig, you need only set the height of the cutter. This is a simple adjustment and normally noncritical.

I have had some difficulty, however, in drilling the holes in the sliding fence that are used to space the cuts. You may have to do this a couple of times to get it just right. Once done, you have it forever.

THE BOX JOINT JIG

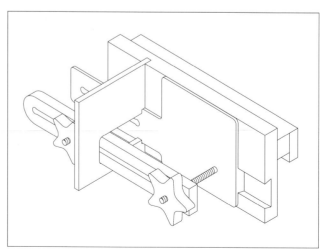

BOX JOINT JIG

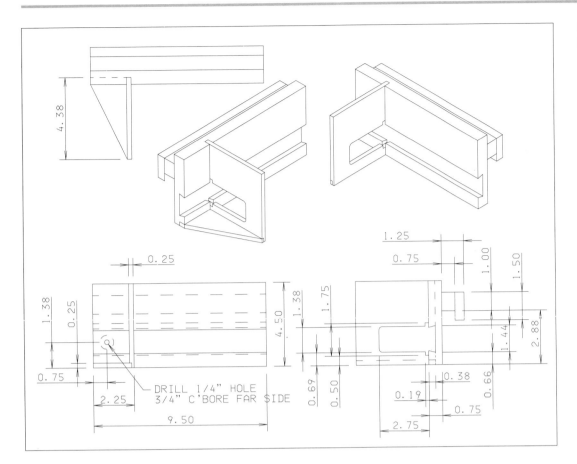

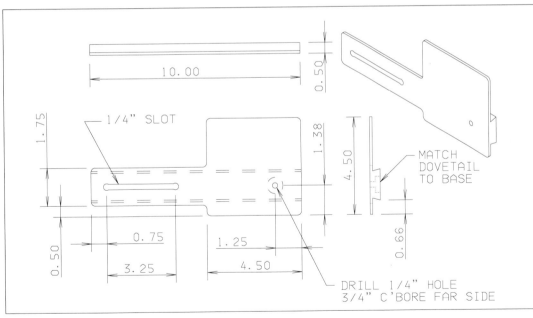

Making the Box Joint Jig

The jig is comprised of two primary pieces, the slide and the base, and a third piece, the clamping bar, which is used to hold the workpieces. The terminology is probably not the best—after the workpieces are clamped in place, the slide remains fixed with respect to the base, and the base is moved along the sliding fence to make the spaced cuts.

The base has a cradle that rides on the sliding fence, a face piece, and a right-angle stop that positions the right sides of the workpieces. A sliding dovetail is cut in the face piece to accept the slide.

To make the slide, start with a piece of ½" Baltic birch plywood cut to 10" x 4½". Cut the slot and then

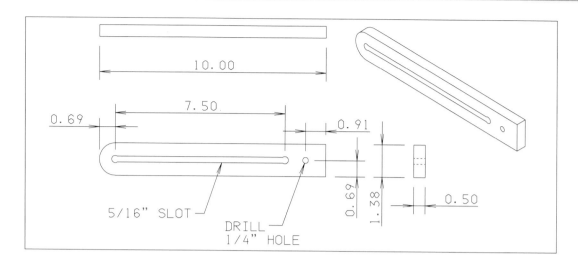

BOX JOINT JIG CLAMPING BAR

cut away the back, leaving a dovetail that matches the dovetail slot in the base. Now cut the slide's outline to its required shape. The ¼" holes in both the base and the slide should be counterbored on the far side to accept the ¼" carriage bolts used to clamp the clamping bar. The final piece is the clamping bar.

Now comes the critical part. The box joint jig must be registered to the sliding fence and a series of ⅛" holes drilled into the top of the sliding fence. The trick is to have these holes spaced at exactly ⅛" and referenced with respect to the router bit. Using a ¼" bit, position the jig so that its right fence is just touching the bit.

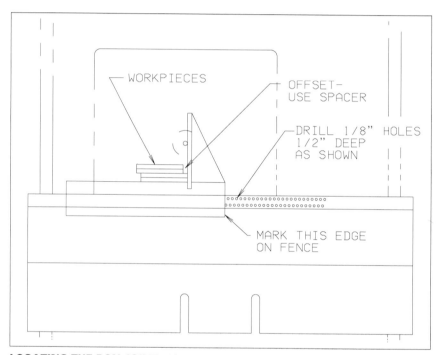

LOCATING THE BOX JOINT JIG STOPS ON THE SLIDING FENCE

Mark the sliding fence at the right edge of the box joint jig. This line is the edge, not the center, of where your ⅛" holes will start. Lay out the holes so that there are two rows, each row having the holes on ¼" centers and offset with respect to the other row by ⅛". This will make the hole layout and drilling easier.

The layout of the holes is best done on paper (use your drafting board). Tape the paper to the sliding fence, then transfer the hole centers to the fence by carefully center punching each hole location. Then drill the holes about ½" deep. An ⅛" drill rod set in the hole is used as a stop for the box joint jig. The particular hole used to start the cutting will depend on the desired spacing and the router bit diameter. Move the drill rod to the next appropriate hole for the next cut

and so forth until all of the pins have been cut. Remember when setting the workpieces in the jig that either the sides or the ends must be offset from the other pair by the width of the workpiece stock (normally the router bit diameter).

The Sliding Vertical Clamp

A sliding vertical clamp is an important accessory for the router workstation. By clamping the sliding fence to the router workstation top, you can use the vertical clamp to perform certain end-cutting operations that are impossible or difficult to perform when the piece is held horizontally. The sliding vertical clamp is shown at right.

The clamp is made from ½" birch plywood and

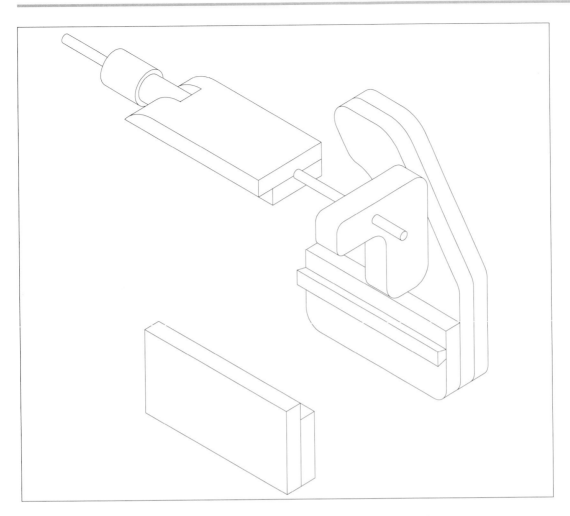

held to the sliding fence with a dovetail strip. This strip can be cut from the strips previously cut. You can use screws or blind dowel joints to hold the various pieces of the clamp together while checking the fit and to facilitate shaping it to its final form. The handle is the same pattern as the saw's push handle.

Clamping of the workpiece is accomplished by permanently attaching a clamp block to a 12" length of ¼" x 20" threaded rod. This rod feeds through the handle part of the clamp assembly. The workpiece is clamped between the front clamp bar and the handled clamp block. The actual clamping is accomplished with a clamp handle made up of two concentric dowels with an embedded nut. If you don't want to go to the trouble of making this clamp

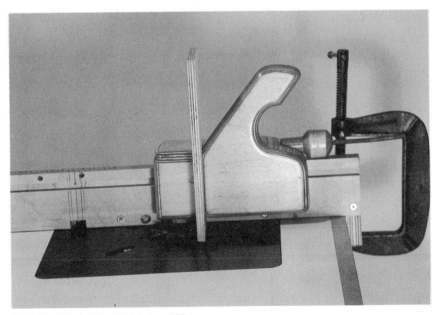

THE SLIDING VERTICAL CLAMP

arrangement, then just make sure that there is a flat face for a nut or wing nut to jam against at the back of the handled block.

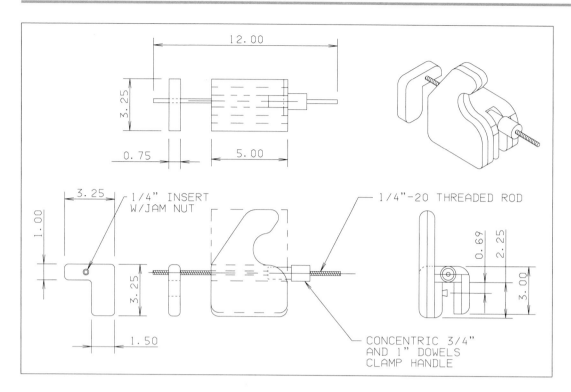

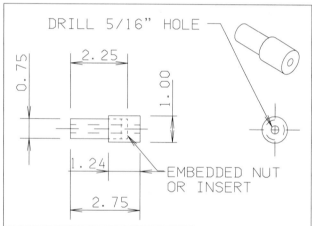

SLIDING VERTICAL CLAMP—CLAMP HANDLE

The Taper Fence

A taper fence can be a handy addition to your router station. The taper of the fence can be cut so that, for a standard vertical displacement, a known horizontal displacement will be made. We have all seen the signs on roads telling us that we are approaching a grade, say a 7 percent grade. This sign is telling us that, as we proceed on the road, for every mile we travel horizontally we will have traveled .07 mile vertically. In other words, the 7 percent tells us the ratio of the X and Y components of the grade. This, of course, is the tangent of the angle of the grade. A 100 percent grade would be 45° slope.

For the taper fence we use the grade or tangent of the taper to allow a known movement of the fence face toward or away from the cutter by moving the sliding portion of the fence a certain distance in the Y direction.

The example here is of a taper fence that uses a taper of 7.1°. The tangent of 7.1° is .125 or $\frac{1}{8}$. What this gives us is a fence that, when moved 8 units in the Y direction, will also move 1 unit in the X direction. In simpler terms, moving the fence 1" vertically will cause the fence to move $\frac{1}{8}$" toward or away from the cutter. Indexing the fence's sliding arm to the fixed arm permits adjustments of $\frac{1}{128}$" to be made by moving the sliding arm 8 times $\frac{1}{128}$", or $\frac{1}{16}$". A sliding dovetail is used to connect the two fence arms. One arm is clamped to the station's top. Normally the fit of the sliding dovetail will allow the sliding arm to be positioned and used without clamping. The dovetail is cut slightly off-center so that the sliding arm will not bind on the top. The fence assembly fits on the top in a manner similar to the sliding fence.

The fence can be made using other taper angles allowing either finer or coarser change (movement away from or toward the cutter). Since the complete fence can be moved with respect to the cutter, I have opted for the rather fine adjustment offered by the 12.5 percent slope or taper.

I use the taper fence most frequently to cut feather-boards. In this application it's used in conjunction with the saber saw mounted in the station. Cutting

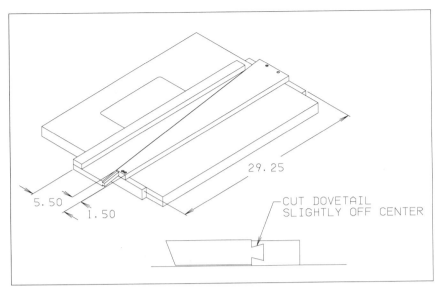

TAPER FENCE

29.25

5.50

1.50

CUT DOVETAIL
SLIGHTLY OFF CENTER

THE TAPER FENCE

the featherboard slots from the center out ensures the firmest edge of the featherboard is riding against the fence. Make the cuts in pairs, turning the workpiece over, for each fence setting. The taper fence can also be used in conjunction with a normal fence for controlling the normal fence's position with respect to the cutter.

MANUFACTURERS

COMPANY	ADDRESS, TELEPHONE	PRODUCT
3M Adhesives Coatings and Sealers Div.	St. Paul, MN 55144 612-733-1110 Operator #55	Spray adhesive
American Tool Companies, Inc.	108 S. Pear St., P.O. Box 337 DeWitte, NE 68341 (402) 683-1525	Quick-Grip clamps
Black & Decker (U.S.) Inc. U.S. Power Tools Group	10 North Park Drive, P.O. Box 798 Hunt Valley, MD 21030-0798 (800) 235-2000	Workmate 300 Work Center
Bridge City Tool Works	1104 N.E. 28th Ave. Portland, OR 97232 800-253-3332	Layout and measuring tools
Delta International Machinery Corp.	246 Alpha Dr. Pittsburgh, PA 15238 (412) 363-8000/(800) 438-2486	30" Unifence
Dick Blick Art Materials	Rt. 150, Knoxville Rd. Galesburg, IL 61401 (800) 447-8192	Drafting Supplies
Eagle Electric Mfg. Co., Inc.	45-31 Court Sq. Long Island City, NY 11101 (718) 937-8000	Clock receptacle
Formica Corp.	155 Route 46, Wayne, NJ 07470 800-524-0159	Plastic laminate
JDS Co.	800 Dutch Square Blvd., Suite 200 Columbia, SC 29210 800-382-2637	Accu-Mitre
Leigh Industries	P.O. Box 357-A, Port Coquitlam B.C. V3C 4K6, Canada	Dovetail jig
Master Magnetics, Inc.	Castle Rock, CO 80104	
Mohawk Finishing Products of Canada	9290 Le Prado, St. Leonard P.Q. H1P 3B4, Canada 800-361-0784	Finishing supplies

COMPANY	ADDRESS, TELEPHONE	PRODUCT
Porter-Cable Corp.	P.O. Box 2468 Jackson, TN 38302 (901) 668-8600	Sanders, routers, router accessories, plate joiners
S-B Tool Company	4300 W. Peterson Chicago, IL 60646 (312) 286-7330	Sanders, routers, router bits Skil and Bosch Tools
Ryobi America Corp.	Pearman Dairy Rd. Anderson, SC 29635 (803) 226-6511	Power tools
Sears, Roebuck and Co.	Sears Tower Chicago, IL 60684 (800) 366-3000	Craftsman tools
Staedtler, Inc.	P.O. Box 2196 Chatsworth, CA 91313 (818) 882-6000	Drafting set used with drafting module
Stanley Tools Works	195 Lake St. New Britain, CT 06050 (203) 225-5111	Tools, hardware
Taylor Design Group, Inc.	P.O. Box 810262 Dallas, TX 75381 (214) 243-7943	Incra Fence, Incra Gauge, Incra Slider
VELCRO USA Inc.	406 Brown Ave. Manchester, NH 03108	Loop and hook products
Willamette Industries, Inc.	KorPINE Div. P.O. Box 1245 Bend, OR 97709 (503) 382-7296	KorTron/EB
Wolfcraft, Inc.	1520 W. Ardmore Ave. Itasca, IL 60143 (708) 773-4777	Dowel Pro

GLOSSARY

amalgamate — To become a homogeneous blend.

back saw — A saw with a metal rib across its back.

bench dog — A metal or wooden peg fitting in holes in a bench surface. Used to retain workpiece.

bond — To cause to adhere firmly. Glue and contact cement are bonding agents.

butch plate — Used to cover or join a mistake.

carcase (also case) — Solid side construction as opposed to frame construction.

chattering — The workpiece vibrating as it is being cut. Results in uneven cuts.

cigar boxes — Any of the small boxes or tins we use to collect the things that are too neat to throw away and, in many cases, that we don't know what to do with.

collet — A tapered sleeve made in two or more segments that grips the shaft of a cutter.

crosscut — To cut across the grain of the wood.

crown moulding — A moulding designed to join two normal surfaces like a room wall and ceiling.

dado — A groove cut in the workpiece.

fence — Any guide used to keep the cutting edge of the tool a fixed distance from the workpiece edge.

ferrule — A metal ring or collar reinforcing the handle of a tool where the tool joins the handle.

hardboard — As used in this book, hardboard means tempered hardboard like that manufactured by Masonite. Use the "Serviced tempered" class of hardboard as defined by the American National Standards Institute (ANSI).

jig — A device to hold the workpiece or the tool so that work can be performed accurately and safely.

KorTron — Industrial particleboard with an electron-beam cured hard, smooth surface. See Willamette Industries, page 147.

laminate — To roll or compress into thin sheet. In this book, the plastic material resulting from this process, like Formica.

MDF — Medium-Density Fiberboard — Particleboard or fiberboard made with fine particles. Works well and finishes well.

miter — A joint formed between two pieces of wood. Usually refers to the gauge or jig used to cut miters.

mussick — A goatskin water bag.

  With 'is mussick on 'is back,
  'E would skip with our attack . . .
  — from "Gunga Din," by Rudyard Kipling, 1865-1936.

noise — Irrelevant or meaningless.

Procrustes — Procrustes had an iron bed on which he compelled his victims to lie, stretching or cutting off their legs to make them fit the bed's length. Also known in Greek legend as Damastes.

Pythagorean theorem — The square of the diagonal (hypotenuse) of a right triangle is equal to the sum of the squares of the lengths of the two sides.

rabbet — A stepped recess along the edge of the workpiece.

rip — To cut with the grain of the wood.

Romex — Insulated copper wire, normally two conductors and one ground wire in a protective plastic or other coating. Used for household wiring.

runners — Normally strips of wood that support and guide drawers or similar structures.

shear panel — Panel structure used to counteract a force applied by a transverse load.

template — A pattern used as a guide.

Theorem of Procrustes — Cut to fit. *See* Procrustes.

INDEX

More Great Books for Your Woodshop!